An-Noor Institute - Essentials

Student Name:	Contact:
Teacher Name:	Contact:

☐ **Level 1: Age 5-9** Start Date:_____ End Date:_____
☐ **Level 2: Age 10-13** Start Date:_____ End Date:_____
☐ **Level 3: Age 14+** Start Date:_____ End Date:_____

Class Checklist

☐ Quran   ☐ Islamic Essentials book
☐ Qaidah   ☐ Notebook
☐ Dua Book   ☐ Pencil

Beloved Parents

➢ Please ensure that your child learns their lessons daily.

➢ Direct your child to perform their daily Salaah.

➢ Constantly remind them of the importance of Islamic dressing and demonstrate this by not buying them any un-Islamic clothes.

➢ Music, smart phones, and television are of great danger and harm to the child's Islamic Tarbiyat and upbringing.

➢ It is our duty to ensure that they are safeguarded from all un-Islamic and immoral influences.

Table of Contents

Title	Subject	Page	Date Completed	Parent's Signature	Teacher's Signature
FIQH	**5 Pillars Of Islam**	8	/ /		
	Shahaadah	9	/ /		
	Conditions of Salaah	11	/ /		
	Istinjaa	12	/ /		
	Ghusl	13	/ /		
	Wudhu	15	/ /		
	Tayammum	17	/ /		
	Adhaan	19	/ /		
	Iqaamah	21	/ /		
SALAAH	**Salaah**	23	/ /		
	Witr Salaah	33	/ /		
	Duaas of Salaah	34	/ /		
	Jumu'ah Salaah	39	/ /		
	Sajdah Tilawat	41	/ /		
	Sajdah Sahw	42	/ /		
	Salaah of a Masbooq	43	/ /		
	Salaah of a Musaafir	44	/ /		
	Salaah of a Mareedh	45	/ /		
	Eid Salaah	46	/ /		
	Janaazah Salaah	48	/ /		
	Duaas of Janaazah Salaah	49	/ /		
	Zakaah	51	/ /		

An-Noor Institute - Essentials of Islam

Title	Subject	Page	Date Completed	Parent's Signature	Teacher's Signature
SAWM	**Sawm**	53	/ /		
	Duas of Sawm	56	/ /		
	I'tikaaf	58	/ /		
	Sadaqatul Fitr	59	/ /		
	Taraweeh Salaah	60	/ /		
HAJJ	**Hajj**	61	/ /		
	Qurbani	65	/ /		
	'Umrah	67	/ /		
	Duaas of Hajj & 'Umrah	68	/ /		
AQEEDAH	Allah	71	/ /		
	The Angels (Malaaikah)	73	/ /		
	The Books of Allah	73	/ /		
	The Messengers of Allah	74	/ /		
	The Sahaabah	76	/ /		
	Fate (Taqdeer)	76	/ /		
	The Last Day (Qiyaamat)	76	/ /		
	The Life After Death	77	/ /		
BASIC ISLAMIC KNOWLEDGE	The 12 Islamic Months	77	/ /		
	Halal & Haram Food	78	/ /		
	The 4 Main Madhabs of Fiqh	79	/ /		
	The 2 Main Madhabs of Aqeedah	79	/ /		
	The 6 Famous Books of Hadith	80	/ /		
	The 3 Holy Cities	80	/ /		
	The Mahram	80	/ /		

An-Noor Institute - Essentials of Islam

Title	Subject	Page	Date Completed	Parent's Signature	Teacher's Signature
100 SUNNAH & ETIQUETTES	Sunnah of Drinking	81	/ /		
	Sunnah of Eating	82	/ /		
	Sunnah of Sleeping	83	/ /		
	Sunnah of Awakening	85	/ /		
	Sunnah of Leaving & Entering the Home	86	/ /		
	Sunnah of Clothing	87	/ /		
	Miscellaneous Sunnah	88	/ /		
	How Should I Spend My Day?	89	/ /		
HADITH	Hadith 1-5	91	/ /		
	Hadith 6-20	92	/ /		
	Hadith 21-40	94	/ /		
SEERAH	**Brief Seerah**	98	/ /		
	The Ahlul Bayt of the Prophet	102	/ /		
	The Characteristics of the Prophet	107	/ /		
	The Last Sermon of the Prophet	110	/ /		
TAJWEED	**Tajweed**	116	/ /		
	The Makhaarij	117	/ /		
	Rules of Full Mouth & Empty Mouth	119	/ /		
	Rules of Waqf (Stopping)	121	/ /		
	Rules of Madd (Stretching)	121	/ /		
	Rules of Ghunnah	123	/ /		

Surah Memorization List

Title	Subject	Date Completed	Subject	Date Completed
SURAH LEVEL 1	Surah Fatiha	/ /	Surah Kafiroon	/ /
	Surah Naas	/ /	Surah Kawthar	/ /
	Surah Falaq	/ /	Surah Maa'oon	/ /
	Surah Ikhlas	/ /	Surah Quraish	/ /
	Surah Lahab	/ /	Surah Feel	/ /
	Surah Nasr	/ /	Surah 'Asr	/ /
SURAH LEVEL 2	Surah Humazah	/ /	Surah Bayyinah	/ /
	Surah Takaathur	/ /	Surah Qadr	/ /
	Surah Qaari-ah	/ /	Surah 'Alaq	/ /
	Surah Aadiyah	/ /	Surah Teen	/ /
	Surah Zilzaal	/ /	Surah Sharh	/ /
SURAH LEVEL 3	Surah Dhuha	/ /	Surah Ghaashiyah	/ /
	Surah Lail	/ /	Surah A'laa	/ /
	Surah Shams	/ /	Surah Taariq	/ /
	Surah Balad	/ /	Surah Burooj	/ /
	Surah Fajr	/ /	Surah Inshiqaaq	/ /
ESSENTIAL SURAHS	Aayatul Kursi	/ /	Surah Yaseen	/ /
	Surah Mulk	/ /	Last 3 Verses of Surah Baqarah	/ /
	Surah Waqi'ah	/ /	Last 3 Verses of Surah Hashr	/ /
	Surah Rahman	/ /	First 10 Verses of Surah Kahaf	/ /
	Surah Sajdah	/ /	Last 10 Verses of Surah Kahaf	/ /

Dua Memorization List

Title	Subject	Date Completed	Subject	Date Completed
DUA LEVEL 1	1st Kalimah Tayyibah	/ /	Dua when awakening	/ /
	2nd Kalimah Shahaadah	/ /	Dua before toilet	/ /
	Greeting a Muslim	/ /	Dua after toilet	/ /
	Reply of the Greeting	/ /	Dua when thanking someone	/ /
	Dua before eating	/ /	Dua when intending to do something	/ /
	Dua when forgetting to read it	/ /	Dua after sneezing	/ /
	Dua after eating	/ /	Dua for increase in knowledge	/ /
	Dua before sleeping	/ /	Dua for parents	/ /
DUA LEVEL 2	3rd Kalimah Tawheed	/ /	Dua after drinking milk	/ /
	4th Kalimah Tamjeed	/ /	Dua when wearing clothes	/ /
	Imaan Mujmal	/ /	Dua when looking into a mirror	/ /
	Imaan Mufassal	/ /	Dua when entering the home	/ /
	Dua before Wudhu	/ /	Dua when leaving the home	/ /
	Dua whilst making Wudhu	/ /	Dua when bidding farewell	/ /
	Dua after Wudhu	/ /	Dua when raining	/ /
	Dua when entering the masjid	/ /	Dua when hearing good news	/ /
	Dua when leaving the masjid	/ /	Dua when a loss occurs	/ /
	Dua after drinking water	/ /	Dua when in difficulty	/ /
DUA LEVEL 3	Dua when getting into a vehicle	/ /	Dua when eating 1st fruit of season	/ /
	Dua when the vehicle moves	/ /	Dua when afflicted with a calamity	/ /
	Dua when returning from journey	/ /	Dua when in financial difficulty	/ /
	Dua when entering a city or town	/ /	Dua when seeing someone in distress	/ /
	Dua when seeing the new moon	/ /	Dua for fever	/ /
	Dua when eating elsewhere (1)	/ /	Dua when visiting the sick	/ /
	Dua when eating elsewhere (2)	/ /	Dua at the time of death	/ /

Reading Syllabus Tracker

Title	Subject	Start Date	End Date	Parent's Signature	Teacher's Signature
QAIDAH	Page 3-10	/ /	/ /		
	Page 11-26	/ /	/ /		
	Page 27-33	/ /	/ /		
	Page 34-48	/ /	/ /		
	Page 49-63	/ /	/ /		
	Page 64-67	/ /	/ /		
	Revision	/ /	/ /		
QURAN READING 1	Surah Zilzaal to Naas	/ /	/ /		
	Surah Balad to Bayyinah	/ /	/ /		
	Surah Inshiqaq to Fajr	/ /	/ /		
	Surah Naba to Mutwaffiffen	/ /	/ /		
	Revision	/ /	/ /		
QURAN READING 2	1st Para	/ /	/ /		
	2nd Para	/ /	/ /		
	3rd Para	/ /	/ /		
	4th Para	/ /	/ /		
	5th Para	/ /	/ /		
	Revision	/ /	/ /		
QURAN READING 3	6th Para - 10th Para	/ /	/ /		
	11th Para - 15th Para	/ /	/ /		
	16th Para - 20th Para	/ /	/ /		
	21th Para - 25th Para	/ /	/ /		
	26th Para - 30th Para	/ /	/ /		
	Revision	/ /	/ /		

FIQH

Definition: Fiqh is a set of rules and laws that have been extracted (taken) and established from the Quran and Hadith.

Status: It is necessary to live our entire lives in accordance with Fiqh.

5 Pillars of Islam

Level 1

Nabi ﷺ said: *"Islam has been built on five [pillars]: testifying that there is none worthy of worship except Allah and that Muhammad is the Messenger of Allah, establishing the Salaah (prayer), paying the Zakaah (obligatory charity), going for Hajj (pilgrimage), and fasting in Ramadhan."*

1. **Shahaadah:** (Declaration of Faith) Every Muslim must believe and declare that there is only one Allah and our Beloved Nabi Muhammad ﷺ is His servant and messenger.

2. **Salaah:** (The 5 daily prayers) Every Muslim must pray to Allah five times every day.

3. **Zakaah:** (Giving to the poor and needy) Once a year, rich Muslims give a small amount of money to the poor Muslims.

4. **Sawm:** (Fasting in the month of Ramadhan) Fasting is to stay away from eating and drinking from Fajr to Sunset.

5. **Hajj:** (Pilgrimage in the month of Dhul Hijjah) Once in a lifetime, Muslims that are able must go to the house of Allah in Makkah to do Hajj.

Shahaadah

KALIMAH TAYYIBAH

لَا إِلٰهَ إِلَّا اللهُ ، مُحَمَّدٌ رَسُولُ اللهِ

Laa-ilaaha illallaahu Muhammadur Rasoolullaah

There is none worthy of worship but Allah and Muhammad ﷺ is the messenger of Allah.

KALIMAH SHAHAADAH (Declaration of Faith)

أَشْهَدُ أَنْ لَا إِلٰهَ إِلَّا اللهُ ، وَأَشْهَدُ أَنَّ مُحَمَّدًا عَبْدُهُ وَرَسُولُهُ

Ash hadu allaa-ilaaha illallaahu wa ash hadu anna Muhammadan 'Abduhoo wa Rasooluh

I testify that there is none worthy of worship but Allah and I testify that Muhammad ﷺ is his servant and messenger.

Level 2

KALIMAH TAWHEED

لَا إِلٰهَ إِلَّا اللهُ ، وَحْدَهُ لَا شَرِيكَ لَهُ ، لَهُ الْمُلْكُ وَلَهُ الْحَمْدُ ، يُحْيِي وَيُمِيتُ ، بِيَدِهِ الْخَيْرُ وَهُوَ عَلَى كُلِّ شَيْءٍ قَدِيرٌ

Laa-ilaaha illallaahu wahdahuu laa shareeka lahuu lahul mulku wa lahul hamdu yuhyee wa yumeetu biyadihil khairu wahuwa 'alaa kulli shai-inn qadeer

There is none worthy of worship but Allah, who is alone and has no partner. For Him is the kingdom and for Him is all praise. He gives life and causes death. In His hand is all good and He has power over everything.

KALIMAH TAMJEED

سُبْحَانَ اللهِ وَالْحَمْدُ لِلَّهِ ، وَلَا إِلَهَ إِلَّا اللهُ وَاللهُ أَكْبَرُ ، وَلَا حَوْلَ وَلَا قُوَّةَ إِلَّا بِاللهِ الْعَلِيِّ الْعَظِيْمِ

Subhaanallaahi walhamdu lillaahi wa laa-ilaaha illallaahu wallaahu akbar walaa hawla walaa quwwata illaa billaahil 'aliyyil 'azheem

Glory be to Allah and all praise belongs to Allah. There is none worthy of worship but Allah and Allah is the greatest. There is no power and might except from Allah, the Most High and Great.

Imaan

Level 1

Definition: Imaan means Faith. To a Muslim, Imaan means firm belief in Allah and the teachings of our Nabi Muhammad ﷺ.

These are the Articles of Faith that all Muslims must believe in:
1. Allah
2. His Angels
3. His Books
4. His Messengers
5. The Last Day
6. Fate: Good and Bad is all from Allah
7. Life after death

Level 2

IMAAN MUJMAL (Imaan in Brief)

أَمَنْتُ بِاللهِ كَمَا هُوَ بِأَسْمَائِهِ وَصِفَاتِهِ ، وَقَبِلْتُ جَمِيْعَ أَحْكَامِهِ

Aamantu billaahi kamaa huwa bi asmaa-ihee wa sifaatihee wa qabiltu jamee'a ahkaamihee

I believe in Allah as He is with His names and His qualities and I accept all His orders.

IMAAN MUFASSAL (Imaan in Detail) The 7 Beliefs of Muslims

أَمَنْتُ بِاللهِ وَمَلَائِكَتِهِ وَكُتُبِهِ وَرُسُلِهِ وَالْيَوْمِ الْآخِرِ وَالْقَدْرِ خَيْرِهِ وَشَرِّهِ مِنَ اللهِ تَعَالَى وَالْبَعْثِ بَعْدَ الْمَوْتِ

Aamantu billaahi wa malaa-ikatihee wa kutubihee wa rusulihee walyawmil aakhiri wal qadri khayrihee wa sharrihee minallaahi ta'aalaa wal ba'thi ba'dal mawt

I believe in Allah, His Angels, His Books, His Messengers, the Last Day, and in Taqdeer, that **all** Good and Bad is from Allah, and I believe in the Resurrection after death.

Conditions of Salaah

Level 1

7 Conditions (Faraaidh) before Salaah:

1. Clean Body
2. Clean Clothes
3. Clean Place
4. Covered Satr
5. Face Qiblah
6. Praying in the Correct Time
7. Making Intention (Niyyah)

1. Clean Body - To clean the body from any impurities by Istinjaa and to be in the state of Wudhu/Ghusl.

2. Clean Clothes - To clean the clothes from any impurities by washing them until there is no trace of impurity.

3. Clean Place - To clean the place from any impurities by washing it until there is no trace of impurity.

4. Covered Satr - The minimum amount that should be covered at all times. For Males: Below the navel to below the knees. For Female (Satr of Salaah): Everything except the face, hands, and feet.

5. Face Qiblah - Qiblah is the direction facing towards the Ka'bah.

6. Praying in the Correct Time - To pray Salaah in their appropriate timings.

7. Making Intention - To intend the form of Salaah for the sake of Allah.

Istinjaa

Level 1

Definition: Istinjaa is to clean and wash the private parts properly after relieving oneself.

Sunan of the Bathroom and Rules of Istinjaa:

1. Do not relieve yourself in a public place or a place that will cause inconvenience to others, rather a place where you cannot be seen.
2. Remove anything with the name of Allah or Quran written on it.
3. Enter the toilet with your head covered. Do not enter bareheaded.
4. Enter the toilet with footwear. Do not enter bare feet.
5. Enter with the left foot and recite the Dua before entering the toilet:

اَللّٰهُمَّ إِنِّيْ أَعُوْذُبِكَ مِنَ الْخُبُثِ وَالْخَبَائِثِ

Allaahumma innee a'oodhubika minal khubuthi wal khabaa-ith

O Allah! I seek refuge in you from the male and female devils.

6. One should not face or show his back towards the Qiblah.
7. To (squat) lower oneself as much as possible before using the toilet.
8. Sit and urinate - One should never urinate whilst standing.
9. Do not read anything, eat, speak, in the toilet. Leave as quickly as possible.
10. Do not read any Quran or Dua in the toilet.
11. Be very careful of splashes and drops of impurity.
12. After urinating, wait until all the drops of urine have come out before making Istinjaa.
13. Use the left hand for making Istinjaa whilst pouring water with the right hand.
14. Use toilet paper, then clean water for Istinjaa.
15. Leave with the right foot and recite the Dua after leaving the toilet:

غُفْرَانَكَ ، اَلْحَمْدُ لِلّٰهِ الَّذِيْ أَذْهَبَ عَنِّي الْأَذَى ، وَعَافَانِيْ

Ghufraanak alhamdulillaahil ladhee adhaba 'annil adhaa wa 'aafaanee

I seek your forgiveness. All praises are due to Allah who has removed my discomfort and granted me relief.

Ghusl

Level 1

Definition: Ghusl means to bathe ourselves in the way shown by Nabi ﷺ with pure and clean water.

Status: It is Fardh (obligatory) to be in the state of Ghusl in order to perform Salaah, recite the Quran, enter the Masjid, or to make Sajdah Tilawat.

3 Faraaidh of Ghusl:

1. Passing water into and out of the mouth (gargling).
2. Putting water into the nostrils.
3. Passing water over the entire body, ensuring no spot is left dry.

5 Sunan of Ghusl:

1. Washing hands up to the wrists.
2. Washing the private parts and the parts over which uncleanliness is found.
3. Niyyah (intention) of washing off Hukmi Najaasah (ritual impurity).
4. Making Wudhu before washing the body.
5. Passing water over the whole body thrice.

Level 2

8 Mustahabbaat of Ghusl:

1. Niyyah (Intention).
2. Ghusl should be made in a private and clean place.
3. Do not face the Qiblah.
4. Better to sit down (but it is alright to do while standing).
5. Do not be stingy or wasteful with the water.
6. Abstain from speaking during Ghusl.
7. No Quran should be recited during Ghusl.
8. It is better to cover your Satr (private area).

The Method of Ghusl:

1. Make an intention to purify oneself from all impurities.
2. Say *Bismillaah* and wash the hands three times until the wrists.
3. Then clean the private parts and other parts where impurities are found.
4. Then do a complete Wudhu, making sure to rinse the mouth and nose three times.
5. Then pour water over the head three times, and rub the water so that the water reaches the roots of the hair. Females do not need to unbraid their hair as long as water reaches the roots of their hair and the base of their head, but males will need to untie their hair and make their hair wet.
6. Then pour water over the right shoulder three times.
7. Rub your body with your hands and make sure the water reaches those places that it cannot reach easily like the armpit, back of knee, navel, etc. Remove anything that will prevent the water from reaching the skin.
8. Then do the same with the left side of your body.
9. Use soap as needed.
10. Wipe your body dry with a towel or leave the body to dry on its own. Both are regarded as Sunnah.

5 Nawaaqidh of Ghusl (Breakers):

1. Wet Dreams.
2. Release of sperm.
3. Haydh (Menstruation/Menses).
4. Nifaas (Post-natal bleeding).
5. Having relations with one's spouse.

Note: Ghusl and Wudhu must be made with clean, pure water. Clean, pure water includes:

- Water that does not have any impurity in it.
- Water that has not been mixed with something so much so that its smell, taste, or color has changed.
- Water that has not been previously used for Wudhu or Ghusl.

Wudhu

Level 1

Definition: Wudhu means to wash ourselves in the way shown by Nabi ﷺ with pure and clean water.

Status: It is Fardh (obligatory) to be in the state of Wudhu before performing Salaah, touching the Quran, making Tawaaf, or making Sajdah Tilawat.

4 Faraaidh of Wudhu:

1. Wash your face once from your hairline to the chin.
2. Wash up to and including your elbows once.
3. Masah (wipe) of at least ¼ of your head once.
4. Wash up to and including your ankles once.

13 Sunan of Wudhu:

1. Niyyah (Intention).
2. Bismillah.
3. Wash both hands until wrists.
4. Miswaak of the teeth.
5. Gargling with water 3 times.
6. Putting water in nose 3 times.
7. Khilaal of the beard.
8. Khilaal of the fingers and toes.
9. Washing of all limbs 3 times.
10. Masah of the whole head.
11. Masah of both ears.
12. Do Wudhu in the correct order.
13. Washing of each part one after another without pause so no part dries up before Wudhu is completed.

Level 2

5 Mustahabbaat of Wudhu:

1. Face the Qiblah.
2. Do Wudhu from the right side.
3. Make Masah on the nape (back of the neck).
4. Do not take help from anyone.
5. Sit in a clean and high place.

8 Nawaaqidh of Wudhu (Breakers):

1. Discharging anything from the private parts.
2. Passing gas.
3. Vomiting a mouthful.
4. Falling into deep sleep by lying down or leaning against something.
5. Becoming unconscious (fainting).
6. Flowing of blood or pus.
7. Becoming insane.
8. Laughing loudly while in any Salaah besides Janaazah Salaah or Sajdah Tilawat.

The Method of Wudhu:

1. Make an intention of purifying oneself from all minor ritual impurities.
2. Recite the Dua before commencing Wudhu.

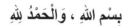

Bismillaahi walhamdulillaah

In the name of Allah and All praises to Allah.

3. Wash **both** the hands upto the wrists three times. The water should reach under the fingernails as well and any nail polish, rings, or anything that prevents the water from reaching the skin should be removed.
4. Clean the teeth with a Miswaak.
5. Use the right hand to gargle three times. The water should reach the top part of the throat.
6. Use the right hand to put water in the nose and the left hand to clean and blow the nose three times.
7. Wash the face from the hairline (where the hair starts to grow) to **below** the chin from one earlobe to the other three times. The eyes and mouth should not be shut so hard that water does not reach the corners of the eyes, the eyelashes, and the lips.
8. Use the right hand to do Khilaal of the beard by passing it through with water. If the beard is not thick, then the water **must** reach the skin.
9. Wash the right arm, starting from the fingers **including** the elbows three times. Then wash the left arm in the same manner.

10. Make Khilaal of the fingers **after** washing the hands by interlacing the fingers of one hand into the other. First the fingers of the left will pass through the right.
11. Then make Masah of the whole head, starting from the forehead till the nape, by wetting your hands, then wiping over the head with the middle fingers, ring fingers, and pinkies.
12. Make Masah of both ears. Wipe the inner portion of the ears with the index fingers and the outer portion with the thumbs.
13. Make Masah of the nape with the back of the fingers and hands.
14. Wash the right foot, starting from the toes **including** the ankles three times. **Then** do Khilaal of the toes by passing the left hand pinky between the toes, starting from the small toes. Then wash the left foot in the same manner.
15. Recite Kalimah Shahaadah and the Dua after completing the Wudhu.

اَللّٰهُمَّ اجْعَلْنِيْ مِنَ التَّوَّابِيْنَ ، وَاجْعَلْنِيْ مِنَ الْمُتَطَهِّرِيْنَ

Allaahummaj'alnee minat tawwaabeena waj'alnee minal mutatwahhireen

O Allah! Make me from the receptors and from the purified ones.

سُبْحَانَكَ اللَّهُمَّ وَبِحَمْدِكَ ، أَشْهَدُ أَنْ لَا إِلَهَ إِلَّا أَنْتَ ، أَسْتَغْفِرُكَ وَأَتُوبُ إِلَيْكَ

Subhaanakllaahumma wabihamdik ash hadu allaa ilaaha illaa anta astaghfiruka wa atoobu ilayka

O Allah, glorified are You and praise be to You. I testify that there is none worthy of worship but You. I seek Your forgiveness and repent to You.

Tayammum

Level 1

Definition: Tayammum means to clean oneself using clean earth, sand, stone, etc., under certain conditions. It is a substitute for Wudhu and Ghusl.

3 Faraaidh of Tayammum:

1. Niyyah (Intention).
2. Striking both hands on earth and rubbing them on the face.
3. Striking both hands on the earth and rubbing both forearms including the elbows.

Conditions of Tayammum:

1. There is no water available within a radius of one mile.
2. There is such a small amount of water left that if it were used up for Wudhu or Ghusl, then there would be a fear of thirst.
3. There is fear of an enemy or dangerous animal by the water.
4. There is a danger to one's health when using water when informed by a reliable doctor.

The Method of Tayammum:

1. Make an intention of purifying oneself with Tayammum on behalf of Wudhu or Ghusl. Niyyah **must** be made.
2. Strike both hands on clean earth or dust and then dust/blow off excess dust.
3. Rub both hands over the entire face **completely**. Ensure no spot is left out. Also make Khilaal of the beard as done in Wudhu.
4. Strike both hands again in the same manner.
5. Rub the right arm **including** the elbow with the left hand. Then rub the left arm. Ensure no spot is left out. Then make Khilaal of the fingers as done in Wudhu.

Note: The same things which break Wudhu and Ghusl will also break Tayammum. And Tayammum will also break if the condition of Tayammum is no longer found.

Note: Tayammum must be made with earth, sand, stone, clay, and all items which have thick dust on them. Tayammum cannot be made on:

- Glass
- Wood
- Metal
- All items which can burn, rot, or melt.

مِفْتَاحُ الْجَنَّةِ الصَّلَاةُ وَمِفْتَاحُ الصَّلَاةِ الْوُضُوْءُ

The Messenger of Allah ﷺ said:

"The key to Paradise is prayer, and the key to prayer is ablution." [Tirmidhi]

Adhaan

Definition: Adhaan is a special way of calling people towards Salaah.

Status: Adhaan is Sunnah Mu'akkadah upon men for the five daily Salaah and Jumu'ah.

Rules of Giving Adhaan:

1. The Muadh-dhin (man calling out the Adhaan) should be in the state of Wudhu when giving the Adhaan and he should be a righteous man.
2. He should face the Qiblah.
3. It is Mustahabb to place the forefingers in the ears when giving the Adhaan.
4. The Adhaan should be called out in a loud and clear voice.
5. The Muadh-dhin should pause between the words of the Adhaan.
6. The Adhaan should be called from outside the boundaries of the Masjid and from a high place, so that the voice can be heard from a distance.
7. The same person should give Iqaamah unless he gives permission to someone else.
8. Sufficient time should be given between Adhaan and Iqaamah for the people to come to the Masjid, except in Maghrib.
9. When saying حَيَّ عَلَى الصَّلٰوةِ the face should be turned to the right. When saying حَيَّ عَلَى الْفَلَاحِ the face should be turned to the left.
    - Only the face should be turned. Not the chest nor the feet.
10. In Fajr Adhaan, اَلصَّلٰوةُ خَيْرٌ مِنَ النَّوْمِ will be said twice after حَيَّ عَلَى الْفَلَاحِ.

The Messenger of Allah ﷺ said: *"If the people knew (the reward of) pronouncing the Adhaan and for standing in the first row in congregational Salaah and found no other way to get that except by drawing lots, then they would draw lots. And if they knew (the reward of) the Dhuhr prayer (in the early moments of its stated time) they would race for it (go early) and if they knew the reward of 'Ishaa and Fajr prayers in congregation, they would come to offer them even if they had to crawl."* [Bukhaari]

Adhaan

اللهُ أَكْبَرُ اللهُ أَكْبَرُ   اللهُ أَكْبَرُ اللهُ أَكْبَرُ

Allah is the greatest.

أَشْهَدُ أَنْ لَّا إِلَهَ إِلَّا الله   أَشْهَدُ أَنْ لَّا إِلَهَ إِلَّا الله

I bear witness that there is no God besides Allah.

أَشْهَدُ أَنَّ مُحَمَّدًا رَّسُوْلُ الله   أَشْهَدُ أَنَّ مُحَمَّدًا رَّسُوْلُ الله

I bear witness that Muhammad is the messenger of Allah.

حَيَّ عَلَى الصَّلٰوة   حَيَّ عَلَى الصَّلٰوة

Come to Salaah. (Turn the face to the right when saying these words)

حَيَّ عَلَى الْفَلَاح   حَيَّ عَلَى الْفَلَاح

Come to success. (Turn the face to the left when saying these words)

اللهُ أَكْبَرُ اللهُ أَكْبَرُ

Allah is the greatest.

لَا إِلَهَ إِلَّا الله

There is no God besides Allah.

The Messenger of Allah said ﷺ: "When the Mu'adhdhin says, 'Allahu Akbar, Allahu Akbar' and you say, 'Allahu Akbar, Allahu Akbar' and when he says, 'Ash-hadu allaa ilaaha illallaah' you say, 'Ash-hadu allaa ilaaha illallaah' and when he says, 'Ash-hadu anna Muhammadar-Rasoolullah' you say, 'Ash-hadu anna Muhammadar-Rasoolah' and when he says, 'Hayya 'alas-Salaah' you say, 'Laa hawla walaa quwwata illaa billaah' and when he says, 'Hayya 'alal falaah' you say, 'Laa hawla walaa quwwata illaa billaah' and when he says, 'Allahu Akbar, Allahu Akbar' you say, 'Allahu Akbar, Allahu Akbar' and when he says, 'Laa ilaaha illallaah' you say from your heart (with sincerity), 'Laa ilaaha illallaah' then you will enter Jannah (Paradise)." [Muslim]

Iqaamah

Definition: A reminder that Salaah is about to commence.

Status: Iqaamah is Sunnah Mu'akkadah upon men for the five daily Salaah and Jumu'ah.

Note: One should not pause between each set of words in the Iqaamah as one does during the Adhaan. Say each line in one breath quickly as it is written here.

Iqaamah

اللهُ أَكْبَرُ اللهُ أَكْبَرُ اللهُ أَكْبَرُ اللهُ أَكْبَرُ

Allah is the greatest.

أَشْهَدُ أَنْ لَا إِلَهَ إِلَّا الله أَشْهَدُ أَنْ لَا إِلَهَ إِلَّا الله

I bear witness that there is no God besides Allah.

أَشْهَدُ أَنَّ مُحَمَّدًا رَسُوْلُ الله أَشْهَدُ أَنَّ مُحَمَّدًا رَسُوْلُ الله

I bear witness that Muhammad is the messenger of Allah.

حَيَّ عَلَى الصَّلوةِ حَيَّ عَلَى الصَّلوةِ

Come to Salaah. (Turn the face to the right when saying these words)

حَيَّ عَلَى الْفَلَاحِ حَيَّ عَلَى الْفَلَاحِ

Come to success. (Turn the face to the left when saying these words)

قَدْ قَامَتِ الصَّلوةُ قَدْ قَامَتِ الصَّلوةُ

Salaah is indeed about to begin.

اللهُ أَكْبَرُ اللهُ أَكْبَرُ

Allah is the greatest.

لَا إِلَهَ إِلَّا الله

There is no God besides Allah.

(Abu Dawud)

Rules of Ijaabah (Replying):

1. One should not talk while the Adhaan and Iqaamah are being called, but rather they should repeat the words of the Muadh-dhin.

2. After أَشْهَدُ أَنَّ مُحَمَّدًا رَسُوْلُ الله, one should also say:

رَضِيْتُ بِاللهِ رَبًّا ، وَبِالْإِسْلَامِ دِيْنًا ، وَبِمُحَمَّدٍ ﷺ رَسُوْلًا وَنَبِيًّا

Radhweetu billaahi rabbaa wabil islaami deenaa wabi muhammadin rasoolaw wanabiyyaa

I am pleased with Allah as my Lord, and Islam as my religion, and with Muhammad ﷺ as my messenger.

3. After حَيَّ عَلَى الصَّلٰوة and حَيَّ عَلَى الْفَلَاح, one should say:

لَا حَوْلَ ، وَلَا قُوَّةَ ، إِلَّا بِاللهِ

Laa Hawla walaa quwwata illaa billaah

There is no power or might, except with Allah.

4. After اَلصَّلٰوةُ خَيْرٌ مِنَ النَّوْمِ, one should say:

قَدْ صَدَقْتَ ، وَبَرَرْتَ

Qadd swadaqqta wa bararta

Verily You have spoken the truth and done good.

5. After قَدْ قَامَتِ الصَّلٰوة, one should say:

أَقَامَهَا اللهُ وَأَدَامَهَا

Aqaamahallaahu wa adaamahaa

May Allah keep the prayers continually established.

6. After the Adhaan, one should read the Dua after Adhaan:

اَللّٰهُمَّ رَبَّ هٰذِهِ الدَّعْوَةِ التَّامَّةِ ، وَالصَّلٰوةِ الْقَائِمَةِ ، آتِ مُحَمَّدًا الْوَسِيْلَةَ ، وَالْفَضِيْلَةَ ، وَابْعَثْهُ مَقَامًا مَحْمُوْدًا الَّذِيْ وَعَدْتَّهُ

Allaahumma rabba haadhihid da'watit taaammah waswalaatil Qaaa-imah aati muhammadanil waseelata wal fadhweelata wab'ath hu maqaamam mahmoodanilladhee wa 'attah

O Allah! Lord of this perfect call and this prayer that is to be established, grant Muhammad Al-Waseelah (a special place in Paradise) and Al-Fadhweelah (a rank above creation) and raise him to a praised station which you promised him.

Salaah
Level 1

Definition: Salaah is a special Ibaadah (worship) that has been commanded by Allah Ta'ala and taught to us by Nabi Muhammad ﷺ.

Status: To perform the five daily Salaah is Fardh (obligatory). To perform in Jamaat (congregation) is Waajib (compulsory) for men.

Salaah is Fardh on:
1. The one who is muslim.
2. The one who is baaligh (reached puberty).
3. The one who is sane.

Rakaats of Salaah:

Fajr	2 Sunnah Mu'akkadah + 2 Fardh = **4 Rakaats**
Dhuhr	4 Sunnah Mu'akkadah + 4 Fardh + 2 Sunnah Mu'akkadah + 2 Nafl = **12 Rakaats**
'Asr	4 Sunnah Ghair-Mu'akkadah + 4 Fardh = **8 Rakaats**
Maghrib	3 Fardh + 2 Sunnah Mu'akkadah + 2 Nafl = **7 Rakaats**
'Ishaa	4 Sunnah Ghair-Mu'akkadah + 4 Fardh + 2 Sunnah Mu'akkadah + 2 Nafl + 3 Witr Waajib + 2 Nafl = **17 Rakaats**
Jumu'ah	4 Sunnah Mu'akkadah + Khutbah + 2 Fardh + 4 Sunnah Mu'akkadah + 2 Sunnah Mu'akkadah + 2 Nafl = **14 Rakaats**
Taraweeh	20 Sunnah Mu'akkadah in sets of 2 = **20 Rakaats**
'Eid	2 Waajib with six extra Takbeers + Khutbah = **2 Rakaats**

6 Faraaidh in Salaah: If you miss any of these, you will have to repeat the Salaah.

1. Takbeer Tahreemah (Raising the Hands, saying اَللهُ أَكْبَر)
2. Qiyaam (Standing Posture)
3. Qiraat (Recitation)
4. Ruku (Bow)
5. Both the Sajdahs (Prostration)
6. Qa'dah Akheerah (Last Sitting Posture)

The Method of Salaah:

1. Takbeer Tahreemah.
2. Recite Thana.
3. Recite Ta'awwudh.
4. Recite Tasmiyah.
5. Recite Surah Fatiha.
6. Recite Tasmiyah.
7. Recite any other Surah.
8. Go into Ruku, saying اَللهُ أَكْبَر.
9. Read the Tasbeeh of Ruku سُبْحَانَ رَبِّيَ الْعَظِيْم at least 3x.
10. Come up from Ruku, saying the Tasmee' سَمِعَ اللهُ لِمَنْ حَمِدَه.
11. Recite the Dua in Qaumah (Tahmeed) رَبَّنَا وَلَكَ الْحَمْد.
12. Go down into Sajdah, saying اَللهُ أَكْبَر.
13. Read the Tasbeeh of Sajdah سُبْحَانَ رَبِّيَ الْأَعْلَى at least 3x.
14. Come up from Sajdah, saying اَللهُ أَكْبَر.
15. Recite the Dua in Jalsah.
16. Go down for the second Sajdah, saying اَللهُ أَكْبَر.
17. Read the Tasbeeh of Sajdah سُبْحَانَ رَبِّيَ الْأَعْلَى at least 3x.
18. Come up from the second Sajdah, saying اَللهُ أَكْبَر and proceed straight into Qiyaam.

YOU HAVE NOW COMPLETED THE FIRST RAKAAT

19. The 2nd Rakaat will be performed in the same manner as the 1st Rakaat. However, Thana and Ta'awwudh will not be recited and you will sit in Qa'dah after the 2nd Sajdah. Recite the following in this Qa'dah:

a) Tashahhud
b) Durood Ibraheem
c) Dua after Durood Ibraheem
d) Make Salaam to the right, saying اَلسَّلَامُ عَلَيْكُمْ وَرَحْمَةُ الله and then to the left, saying اَلسَّلَامُ عَلَيْكُمْ وَرَحْمَةُ الله.

20. If you are performing 3 or 4 Rakaats, you will only read Tashahhud in the first sitting and continue.

Note:

1. If you are performing three or four Rakaats of a Fardh Salaah, then only Surah Fatiha will be recited in the 3rd and 4th Rakaats.
2. If you are performing Salaah behind the Imaam, you will not recite Surah Fatiha or any Surah in any of the Rakaats. The Imaam's Qiraat suffices as your Qiraat.
3. If you miss any Fardh or Waajib Salaah, **you will have to make it up** (Qadha). Intentionally missing **any** Salaah is a major sin.

Level 2

14 Waajibaat of Salaah: If you miss any of these mistakenly, you will have to perform Sajdah Sahw but if you do not perform Sajdah Sahw or you miss any of these knowingly, you will have to repeat the Salaah.

1. To recite after Surah Fatiha in the first two Rakaats of Fardh Salaah.
2. To recite Surah Fatiha in all Rakaats of every Salaah, except the 3rd and 4th Rakaats of Fardh Salaah where it is Sunnah.
3. To recite at least three short aayaat or one long aayat after Surah Fatiha in the first two Rakaats of Fardh Salaah and in **all** Rakaats of all other Salaah.
4. To recite Surah Fatiha first before the other Surah.
5. To maintain order between Qiyaam, Ruku, Sajdah, and the Rakaats.
6. Qaumah (to stand after Ruku).
7. Jalsah (to sit between both Sajdahs).
8. Ta'deel Arkaan (to perform Salaah calmly and slowly).
9. Qa'dah Oola (First sitting posture).
10. To read Tashahhud in both Qa'dahs.
11. Imaam to recite Qiraat aloud in the first two Rakaats of Fajr, Maghrib, 'Ishaa, Jumu'ah, 'Eid, Taraweeh, and Witr (Ramadhan only).
12. To complete the Salaah by saying Salaam.
13. To say Takbeer in the 3rd Rakaat of Witr Salaah and to recite Dua Qunoot.
14. To say six additional Takbeers in 'Eid Salaah.

21 Sunan of Salaah:

1. To raise the hands up to the ears before saying Takbeer Tahreemah.
2. To keep the fingers raised and palms facing the Qiblah during Takbeer.
3. Not to bend the head while performing Takbeer.
4. To say Takbeer Tahreemah and all other takbeers aloud by the Imaam.
5. To place the right hand over the left hand under the navel.
6. To recite Thana at the beginning of the first Rakaat.
7. To recite Ta'awwudh after Thana.
8. To recite Tasmiyah at the beginning of every Rakaat.
9. To recite Surah Fatiha only in the 3rd and 4th Rakaat of Fardh Salaah.
10. To say *Aameen* after Surah Fatiha.
11. To recite Thana, Ta'awwudh, Tasmiyah, and Aameen softly.
12. To recite the Sunnah Qiraat portions.
    - Fajr and Dhuhr: Surah Hujuraat to Surah Inshiqaaq
    - 'Asr and 'Ishaa: Surah Burooj to Surah Qadr
    - Maghrib: Surah Bayyinah to Surah Naas
13. To keep the back and head at the same level while holding the knees in Ruku.
14. To say the Tasbeeh at least three times in Ruku and Sajdah.
15. For the Imaam to say Tasmee' and the Muqtadees (followers) to say Tahmeed. The Munfarid should read both.
16. To place the knees first, then the palms, then the nose, and then the forehead when going for Sajdah.
17. To place the left foot horizontally and to sit on it and to raise the right foot vertically with the toes towards Qiblah and the hands on the thighs in Qa'dah and Jalsah.
18. To raise the index finger of the right hand as one says *Ash hadu Allaa ilaaha* in Tashahhud.
19. To recite Durood Ibraheem after Tashahhud.
20. To recite the Dua after Durood Ibraheem.
21. To turn the face to the right and left for Salaam while making Intention for the angels and other muslims praying.

Level 3

Mufsidaat of Salaah (Nullifiers):

1. To talk in Salaah, knowingly or unknowingly.
2. To make a sound or noise, due to pain or any other reason.
3. To give or reply to Salaam verbally or any other method.
4. To reply to one who has sneezed or to say *Aameen* to a Dua not connected to the Salaah.
5. To say the Dua after hearing sad news or to say *Alhamdulillah* or *Subhanallah* after hearing good news.
6. To correct the recitation of someone other than the Imaam.
7. To recite the Quran by looking at the text.
8. To make a major mistake in the recitation that will change the meaning into a statement of disbelief, without immediately correcting it.
9. To do such actions which gives others the impression that he is not in Salaah.
10. To eat or drink, knowingly or unknowingly.
11. To turn the chest away from Qiblah without a valid excuse.
12. To leave at least 1/4th of the Satr uncovered for the duration of three *Subhanallah*s.
13. To laugh aloud (breaks Wudhu also).
14. To perform Sajdah at an impure place.
15. To go ahead of the Imaam in a Fardh Salaah.
16. To walk the extent of two rows.

Prohibited times of Salaah:

1. At Sunrise
2. At Midday (Istiwaa)
3. At Sunset

Disliked times of Salaah:

1. After Fajr Salaah till sunrise.
2. After 'Asr Salaah till sunset.

Times of Salaah:

Fajr	From Subh Saadiq (early dawn) till before sunrise.
Dhuhr	From Zawaal (past noon) (after Istiwaa) till the shadow of an object becomes twice its length plus its original midday shadow.
'Asr	From after Dhuhr till little before sunset.
Maghrib	From after sunset till the redness in the horizon has faded away.
'Ishaa	From after Maghrib till Fajr but it is undesirable to delay it after midnight.
Jumu'ah	From Dhuhr time till 'Asr time during Friday.
Taraweeh	From after 'Ishaa till a little before Fajr time during the month of Ramadhan.
'Eid	Eid-ul-Fitr is after Ramadhan (1st of Shawwaal) and Eid-ul-Adha is after Hajj (10th of Dhul Hijjah) from sunrise to Istiwaa.

Types of Nafl (Optional) Salaah:

1. Tahiyatul Masjid - 2 Rakaats performed after entering the Masjid, preferably before sitting down.
2. Tahiyatul Wudhu - 2 Rakaats performed after completing Wudhu.
3. Ishraaq Salaah - 2 or 4 Rakaats performed 20 minutes after sunrise.
4. Dhuha Salaah - 2 or 4 (upto 12) Rakaats performed after midmorning (Ishraaq) till the time of Dhuhr.
5. Awwaabeen Salaah - 6 Rakaats performed between Maghrib and 'Ishaa.
6. Tahajjud Salaah - In the night, performed anytime from after 'Ishaa till Fajr.
7. Tawbah Salaah - Salaah performed to seek forgiveness from Allah.
8. Haajah Salaah - Salaah performed to seek Allah's help for any need.
9. Istikhaarah Salaah - Salaah performed to seek Allah's blessing when making an important decision.

The Detailed Method of Salaah:

1. Before Salaah:

1. He should make sure all 7 conditions before Salaah are fulfilled.
2. He should ensure that he is not hungry nor in need of going to the toilet. He should take care of his needs and do Wudhu at home before going to the Masjid.
3. He should ensure that there are no bad or strong smells coming out from the body or mouth like the smell of cigarettes or garlic, etc.
4. He should wear such clothes that are loose with his sleeves till his wrists and pants above his ankles. He should not wear any clothing 1) that are tight fitting or the shape of the body becomes apparent, 2) that are not worn in the presence of respectable people, 3) that resemble the clothing of the sinful people or disbelievers.
5. He should not rush or run to Salaah.
6. He should not pray in such a place that will disturb others like a pathway nor in such a place where there are pictures or animated designs.
7. He should straighten the line by having his heel in line with the next person. It is not necessary to join his feet with the next person's feet.
8. He should keep his hands to his sides. He should not crack his fingers or fold his arms, etc. nor look around.
9. He should keep his feet straight with his toes facing the Qiblah.
10. He should try and concentrate in Salaah. He should think that this is his last Salaah and Allah is watching him.

2. Takbeer Tahreemah:

11. He should raise his hands to his ears and while dropping and folding his hands, he should say اللهُ أَكْبَر.
12. The palms should face the Qiblah and the fingertips should point upwards.
13. The fingers should be in a natural position, not too close or too far.
14. The head should not be lowered or raised and the back should also be kept upright.
15. Females should raise their hands to their shoulders without exposing their hands.

3. Qiyaam:

16. Then place the right palm on top of the left hand below the navel (belly button).
17. Form a circle around the left wrist with the thumb and pinky of the right hand, leaving the middle three fingers on the left forearm.
18. Keep the feet a normal distance apart, not too close or too far and they should continue facing the Qiblah.
19. He should keep his gaze at the place of Sajdah. He should not look around.
20. Females should keep their feet together and tie their hands on their chest with the right palm on the back of their left hand.

4. Qiraat:

21. Qiraat must be recited with proper Tajweed at all times.
22. If the same Surah is recited in both Rakaats, the Salaah is valid but one should not do this unnecessarily.
23. The Qiraat of the first Rakat should be longer than the Qiraat of the second Rakaat.
24. The Qiraat of the first Rakat should be before the Qiraat of the second Rakat in terms of the order and sequence in the Quran.
25. Females should always recite silently.

5. Ruku:

26. Grab the knees with the hands keeping the fingers spread apart.
27. He should keep his gaze fixed at his feet.
28. Keep the back and the head straight and inline with each other.
29. Keep the arms straight. The elbows should not be bent.
30. Females should only bow down so much that their hands are able to touch their knees with their fingers and feet kept apart and their elbows touching their sides.

6. Qaumah:

31. Stand completely (with ease) before going to Sajdah. Do not rush to Sajdah.
32. The hands should be kept to the side in a natural position. The hands should not be clenched in a fist.
33. Say the Takbeer while going to Sajdah, not before or after.
34. When going down, first place the knees on the ground, then the hands, then the nose, and lastly the forehead.
35. Females should stand in a similar way.

7. Sajdah:

36. The fingers should be kept together with no gap and level with the ears and the gaze fixed on the nose.
37. The arms should be away from the sides and the elbows should be off the ground and there should be a gap between the stomach and thighs.
38. The feet should be kept together and the toes should be bent facing the Qiblah. The feet and forehead should **not** lift from the ground.
39. When getting up, first raise the forehead, then the nose, then the hands, and lastly the knees. This is opposite to when going down.
40. Females should keep their stomach and thighs together, with their arms flat on the ground and their feet (horizontally) flat facing the right.

8. Qa'dah:

41. Keep the left foot flat on the ground and sit on it with the right foot upright. The toes of both feet should face the Qiblah. Men must sit in all sittings in this position (including Jalsah).
42. Keep the gaze fixed on the lap with the head and back straight.
43. Place both the hands on the thighs just above the knees with the fingers in their natural position, not too close or too far.
44. In Tashahhud, when saying the words أَشْهَدُ أَنْ لَا إِلٰهَ, form a ring with the middle finger and thumb and raise the index finger towards the Qiblah. Lower the finger when saying إِلَّا اللهُ, but the ring should be kept till Salaam.
45. Females should sit on the floor with their feet flat on their right side.

9. Salaam:

46. Begin the first Salaam with the face in the direction of the Qiblah and complete it when the face is fully turned to the right. Then begin the second Salaam with the face in the direction of the Qiblah again.
47. Do not dip or bow the head.
48. Keep the gaze on the shoulders and make Niyyah of greeting the angels.
49. The Imaam should say the second Salaam in a softer tone than the first.
50. Females should give Salaam in a similar way without raising their voices.

10. After Salaah:

51. Recite the Duaas after Salaah.
52. Recite Tasbeeh Fatimi (33 x 'SubhanAllaah', 33 x 'Alhamdulillaah', 34 x 'Allaahu Akbar') and Kalimah Tawheed.
53. Recite Aayatul Kursi.
54. Recite Surah Ikhlas, Surah Falaq, and Surah Naas. These three Surahs should be recited three times each after Fajr and Maghrib.
55. Recite any and all Duaas one knows and to ask Allah for one's needs.

11. General

56. Read Salaah slowly and do not rush the positions.
57. The Takbeer should be said while moving from position to position for the duration of the movement.
58. It is not necessary to make Niyyah verbally, but Niyyah must be made in the mind.
59. The Imaam needs to have Niyyah of leading, otherwise the Salaah of those following him will be invalid. Likewise, those following him need to have Niyyah of following him.
60. Lengthen the Salaah performed individually.

Witr Salaah
Level 1

Definition: Witr Salaah is a 3 Rakaat Salaah which is performed after the Fardh of 'Ishaa. It cannot be performed before the Fardh of 'Ishaa.

Status: Waajib (compulsory)

The Method of Witr Salaah:

There are 3 Rakaats in the Witr Salaah which are performed as follows:

- Pray **1st & 2nd Rakaat** as normal.

- **3rd Rakaat:** After the Qiraat, lift both hands up to the ears, saying اللهُ أَكْبَر and then fold them. Thereafter recite Dua Qunoot. After Dua Qunoot, go into Ruku and complete the Salaah as normal.

SALAH

Duaas of Salaah
Level 1

1. Thana

سُبْحَانَكَ اللّٰهُمَّ وَبِحَمْدِكَ ، وَتَبَارَكَ اسْمُكَ ، وَتَعَالَى جَدُّكَ ، وَلَا إِلٰهَ غَيْرُكَ

Subhaanaka Allaahumma wabi hamdika wata-baara kasmuka wata'aalaa jadduka walaa ilaaha ghayruka.

O Allah, glorified are You and praise be to You. Blessed is Your name, and exalted is Your majesty. There is no one worthy of worship but You.

2. Dua in Jalsah

اَللّٰهُمَّ اغْفِرْ لِيْ ، وَارْحَمْنِيْ ، وَعَافِنِيْ ، وَاهْدِنِيْ ، وَارْزُقْنِيْ

Allaahummagh firlee warhamnee wa 'aafinee wahdinee warzuqqnee

O Allah, forgive me, have mercy on me, protect me, guide me, and grant me sustenance.

3. Tashahhud

التَّحِيَّاتُ لِلّٰهِ وَالصَّلَوَاتُ وَالطَّيِّبَاتُ ، السَّلَامُ عَلَيْكَ أَيُّهَا النَّبِيُّ وَرَحْمَةُ اللهِ وَبَرَكَاتُهُ ، السَّلَامُ عَلَيْنَا وَعَلَى عِبَادِ اللهِ الصَّالِحِيْنَ ، أَشْهَدُ أَنْ لَّا إِلٰهَ إِلَّا اللهُ ، وَأَشْهَدُ أَنَّ مُحَمَّدًا عَبْدُهُ وَرَسُوْلُهُ

Attahiyyaatu lillaahi was swalawaatu wattwayyibaatu assalaamu 'alaika ayyuhannabiyyu warahmatullahi wabarkaatuhu assalamu 'alaina wa 'alaa 'ibaadillaahis swaaliheen, ash hadu allaa ilaaha illallaahu wa ash hadu anna Muhammadan 'abduhuu wa rasooluh

All greetings, prayers and goodness belong to Allah. Peace be upon you O Prophet and the mercy of Allah and His blessings. Peace be upon us and upon the righteous slaves of Allah. I bear witness that none has the right to be worshiped except Allah, and I bear witness that Muhammad ﷺ is His slave and messenger.

4. Durood Ibraheem

اَللّٰهُمَّ صَلِّ عَلَى مُحَمَّدٍ وَعَلَى آلِ مُحَمَّدٍ ، كَمَا صَلَّيْتَ عَلَى إِبْرَاهِيْمَ وَعَلَى آلِ إِبْرَاهِيْمَ ، إِنَّكَ حَمِيْدٌ مَجِيْدٌ ، اَللّٰهُمَّ بَارِكْ عَلَى مُحَمَّدٍ وَعَلَى آلِ مُحَمَّدٍ ، كَمَا بَارَكْتَ عَلَى إِبْرَاهِيْمَ وَعَلَى آلِ إِبْرَاهِيْمَ ، إِنَّكَ حَمِيْدٌ مَجِيْدٌ

Allaahumma swalli 'alaa Muhammadin wa 'alaa aali Muhammadin kamaa swallayta 'alaa Ibraaheema wa 'alaa aali Ibraaheema innaka Hameedum Majeed
Allahumma baarik 'alaa Muhammadin wa 'alaa aali Muhammadin kamaa baarakta 'alaa Ibraaheema wa 'alaa aali Ibraaheema Innaka Hameedum Majeed

O Allah send peace on Nabi Muhammad ﷺ and to the family of Nabi Muhammad ﷺ as You sent peace on Prophet Ibraheem AS and the family of Prophet Ibraheem AS. Indeed, You are Praiseworthy and Glorious.
O Allah, bless the Nabi Muhammad ﷺ and the family of Nabi Muhammad ﷺ as you blessed Prophet Ibraheem AS and the family of Prophet Ibraheem AS. Indeed, You are Praiseworthy and Glorious.

5. Dua after Durood Ibraheem

اَللّٰهُمَّ إِنِّيْ ظَلَمْتُ نَفْسِيْ ظُلْمًا كَثِيْرًا ، وَلَا يَغْفِرُ الذُّنُوْبَ إِلَّا أَنْتَ ، فَاغْفِرْ لِيْ مَغْفِرَةً مِنْ عِنْدِكَ وَارْحَمْنِيْ ، إِنَّكَ أَنْتَ الْغَفُوْرُ الرَّحِيْمُ

Allaahumma innee zhalamtu nafsee zhulmann katheeraa, wa laa yaghfirutdh dhunooba illaa anta, faghfir lee maghfiratam min 'indika warhamnee innaka antal ghafoorur raheem

O Allah, I have greatly wronged myself, and no one forgives sins but You. So grant me forgiveness and have mercy on me. Surely, You are the Most Forgiving, Most Merciful.

6. Dua Qunoot

اَللّٰهُمَّ إِنَّا نَسْتَعِيْنُكَ وَ نَسْتَغْفِرُكَ ، وَ نُؤْمِنُ بِكَ ، وَ نَتَوَكَّلُ عَلَيْكَ وَنُثْنِيْ عَلَيْكَ الْخَيْرَ ، وَ نَشْكُرُكَ وَلَا نَكْفُرُكَ ، وَ نَخْلَعُ وَ نَتْرُكُ مَنْ يَفْجُرُكَ ، اَللّٰهُمَّ إِيَّاكَ نَعْبُدُ وَ لَكَ نُصَلِّيْ وَ نَسْجُدُ ، وَ إِلَيْكَ نَسْعٰى وَ نَحْفِدُ ، وَ نَرْجُوْ رَحْمَتَكَ وَ نَخْشٰى عَذَابَكَ ، إِنَّ عَذَابَكَ بِالْكُفَّارِ مُلْحِقٌ

Allaahumma innaa nasta'eenuka wa nastaghfiruka. Wa nu-minu bika wa natawwakkalu 'alayka wa nuthnee 'alaykal khayra wa nashkuruka wa laa nakfuruk. Wa nakhla'u wa natruku may yaf juruk. Allaahumma iyyaaka na'budu wa laka nuswallee wa nasjudu wa ilayka nas'aa wa nahfidu wa narjuu rahmataka wa nakhshaa 'adhaabaka inna 'adhaabaka bil kuffaari mulhiq

O Allah! We seek Your help and we seek Your forgiveness and believe in You and rely on You and praise You and we are thankful to You and are not ungrateful to You and we forsake and leave those who disobey You. O Allah! You alone do we worship and for You do we pray and prostrate and we run to You and present ourselves for the service in Your cause and we hope for Your mercy and fear Your punishment. Indeed, Your punishment is going to join disbelievers.

7. Alternative Dua for Qaumah

رَبَّنَا وَلَكَ الْحَمْدُ مِلْءَ السَّمَاوَاتِ وَالْأَرْضِ وَمِلْءَ مَا بَيْنَهُمَا وَمِلْءَ مَا شِئْتَ مِنْ شَىْءٍ بَعْدُ

Rabbanaa walakal hamdu mil-as samaawaati wal-ardhwi wa mil-a maa baynahumaa wamil-a maa shi-ta min shai-imm ba'du

Allah listens to him who praises Him. O our lord, and all praises be to Thee in the whole of the heavens and the earth, and what is between them, and in whatever Thou creates afterwards.

8. Alternative Duaas for Ruku & Sajdah

سُبْحَانَكَ اللّٰهُمَّ رَبَّنَا ، وَبِحَمْدِكَ ، اَللّٰهُمَّ اغْفِرْ لِيْ

Subhaanakallaahumma rabbanaa wa bihammdika Allaahummaghfirlee

Glorified are You, O Allah, our Lord. And praise be to You. O Allah! Forgive me.

سُبُّوْحٌ ، قُدُّوسٌ ، رَبُّ الْمَلَائِكَةِ وَالرُّوْحِ

Subbooh quddoos Rabbul malaa-ikati warrooh

You are the Most Glorious, the Most Holy, and the Lord of the angels and the Spirit (Jibraeel).

سُبْحَانَ ذِي الْجَبَرُوْتِ وَالْمَلَكُوْتِ وَالْكِبْرِيَآءِ وَالْعَظَمَةِ

Subhaana dhil jabarooti wal malakooti wal kibriyaa-i wal 'azhwamah

Glorified are You, Master of Power, Dominion, of Majesty and Greatness.

9. Duaas after Salaah

اللهُ أَكْبَر ، أَسْتَغْفِرُ الله أَسْتَغْفِرُ الله أَسْتَغْفِرُ الله ، اَللّٰهُمَّ أَنْتَ السَّلَامُ ، وَمِنْكَ السَّلَامُ ، تَبَارَكْتَ يَا ذَا الْجَلَالِ وَالْإِكْرَامِ

Allaahu Akbar Astaghfirullaah Astaghfirullaah Astaghfirullaah Allaahumma antas salaam wa minkas salaam tabaarakta yaa dhal jalaali wal ikraam

Allah is the greatest. I ask Allah for forgiveness three times. O Allah! You are peace and peace comes from You. Blessed You are, O Possessor of Glory and Honor.

لَا إِلَهَ إِلَّا اللهُ ، وَحْدَهُ لَا شَرِيْكَ لَهُ ، لَهُ الْمُلْكُ وَلَهُ الْحَمْدُ ، وَهُوَ عَلَى كُلِّ شَيْءٍ قَدِيْرٌ ، وَلَا حَوْلَ وَلَا قُوَّةَ إِلَّا بِاللهِ الْعَلِيِّ الْعَظِيْمِ ، لَا إِلَهَ إِلَّا اللهُ ، لَهُ النِّعْمَةُ وَلَهُ الْفَضْلُ وَلَهُ الثَّنَاءُ الْحَسَنُ ، لَا إِلَهَ إِلَّا اللهُ ، مُخْلِصِيْنَ لَهُ الدِّيْنَ وَلَوْ كَرِهَ الْكَافِرُوْنَ

Laa-ilaaha illallaahu wahdahuu laa shareeka lahuu lahul mulku wa lahul hamdu wahuwa 'alaa kulli shai-inn qadeer walaa hawla walaa quwwata illaa billaahil 'aliyyil 'azheem Laa-ilaaha illallaahu lahun ni'matu walahul fadhlu walahuth thanaa-ul hasan Laa-ilaaha illallaahu mukhlisweena lahuddeena walaw karihal kaafiroon

There is none worthy of worship but Allah, who is alone and has no partner. For Him is the kingdom and for Him is all praise. He has power over everything. There is no power and might except from Allah, the Most High and Great. There is none worthy of worship but Allah. For Him is all favor, grace, and glorious praise. There is none worthy of worship but Allah and we are sincere in faith and devotion to Him, even if the disbelievers detest it.

لَا إِلَهَ إِلَّا اللهُ ، وَحْدَهُ لَا شَرِيْكَ لَهُ ، لَهُ الْمُلْكُ وَلَهُ الْحَمْدُ ، وَهُوَ عَلَى كُلِّ شَيْءٍ قَدِيْرٌ ، اَللَّهُمَّ لَا مَانِعَ لِمَا أَعْطَيْتَ ، وَلَا مُعْطِيَ لِمَا مَنَعْتَ ، وَ لَا يَنْفَعُ ذَا الْجَدِّ ، مِنْكَ الْجَدُّ

Laa-ilaaha illallaahu wahdahuu laa shareeka lahuu lahul mulku wa lahul hamdu wahuwa 'alaa kulli shai-inn qadeer Allaahumma laa maani'a limaa aa'twata wa laa mu'twiya limaa mana'ta wa laa yanfa'u dhal jaddi minkal jadd

There is none worthy of worship but Allah, who is alone and has no partner. For Him is the kingdom and for Him is all praise. He has power over everything. O Allah! None can prevent what You have willed to bestow and none can bestow what You have willed to prevent. No wealth can benefit anyone, because all wealth and majesty is from You.

اَللَّهُمَّ أَعِنِّيْ عَلَى ذِكْرِكَ ، وَشُكْرِكَ ، وَحُسْنِ عِبَادَتِكَ

Allaahumma innee a'innee 'alaa dhikrika wa shukrika wa husni 'ibaadatik

O Allah! Assist me in remembering you, and being grateful to you, and performing Your worship in an excellent manner.

Jumu'ah Salaah

Level 1

Definition: Jumu'ah Salaah is performed every Friday instead of Dhuhr after the Imaam gives a Khutbah (speech).

Status: To perform the Jumu'ah Salaah is Fardh (obligatory).

Jumu'ah Salaaah is Fardh on:

1. The one who is muslim.
2. The one who is male.
3. The one who is baaligh.
4. The one who is sane.
5. The one who is free.
6. The one who is healthy.
7. The one who is not traveling.
8. The one who is not living in a small village where no Jumu'ah Salaah is not being performed.

Level 2

Sunan of the Day of Jumu'ah:

1. Cleanse your mouth using the Miswaak.
2. Clip your nails and remove extra hair.
3. Take a Ghusl.
4. Dress in your best clothing (i.e. the best clothing in your possession, not necessarily new clothing).
5. Apply 'Itr (perfume) and oil (to your hair).
6. Reading Surah Kahaf for protection against Dajjal and an illuminating light.
7. To go to the Masjid early and pray as close to the front as possible (without pushing or separating people).
8. Listening to the Khutbah attentively. (One should not talk, read Quran, or even pray while the Khutbah is going on.)
9. To send abundant salutations and Durood upon Rasulullah ﷺ throughout the day.
10. To supplicate and make dua to Allah abundantly throughout the day, especially between the two Khutbahs, and between 'Asr and Maghrib Salaah.

Level 3

The First Khutbah — اَلْخُطْبَةُ الْأُولَى

اَلْحَمْدُ لِلهِ الَّذِيْ هَدَانَا لِهَذَا. وَمَا كُنَّا لِنَهْتَدِيَ لَوْلَا أَنْ هَدَانَا اللهُ. وَنَشْهَدُ أَنْ لَا إِلَهَ إِلَّا اللهُ وَحْدَهُ لَا شَرِيْكَ لَهُ. وَنَشْهَدُ أَنَّ مُحَمَّدًا عَبْدُهُ وَرَسُوْلُهُ. وَصَلَّى اللهُ عَلَيْهِ وَعَلَى آلِهِ وَأَصْحَابِهِ. **أَمَّا بَعْدُ.**

فَيَا أَيُّهَا النَّاسُ. وَحِّدُوا اللهَ فَإِنَّ التَّوْحِيْدَ رَأْسُ الطَّاعَاتِ. وَاتَّقُوا اللهَ فَإِنَّ التَّقْوَى مِلَاكُ الْحَسَنَاتِ. وَعَلَيْكُمْ بِالسُّنَّةِ فَإِنَّ السُّنَّةَ تَهْدِيْ إِلَى الْإِطَاعَةِ وَمَنْ أَطَاعَ اللهَ وَرَسُوْلَهُ فَقَدْ رَشَدَ وَاهْتَدَى. وَإِيَّاكُمْ وَالْبِدْعَةَ فَإِنَّ الْبِدْعَةَ تَهْدِيْ إِلَى الْمَعْصِيَةِ وَمَنْ يَعْصِي اللهَ وَرَسُوْلَهُ فَقَدْ ضَلَّ وَغَوَى. وَعَلَيْكُمْ بِالصِّدْقِ فَإِنَّ الصِّدْقَ يُنْجِيْ وَالْكَذِبَ يُهْلِكُ. وَعَلَيْكُمْ بِالْإِحْسَانِ فَإِنَّ اللهَ يُحِبُّ الْمُحْسِنِيْنَ. وَلَا تُحِبَّ الدُّنْيَا فَتَكُوْنُوا مِنَ الْخَاسِرِيْنَ. أَلَا وَإِنَّ نَفْسًا لَنْ تَمُوْتَ حَتَّى تَسْتَكْمِلَ رِزْقَهَا. فَاتَّقُوا اللهَ وَأَجْمِلُوا فِي الطَّلَبِ وَتَوَكَّلُوا عَلَيْهِ فَإِنَّ اللهَ يُحِبُّ الْمُتَوَكِّلِيْنَ. وَادْعُوْهُ فَإِنَّ رَبَّكُمْ مُجِيْبُ الدَّاعِيْنَ. أَعُوْذُ بِاللهِ مِنَ الشَّيْطَانِ الرَّجِيْمِ. وَقَالَ رَبُّكُمْ ادْعُوْنِيْ أَسْتَجِبْ لَكُمْ إِنَّ الَّذِيْنَ يَسْتَكْبِرُوْنَ عَنْ عِبَادَتِيْ سَيَدْخُلُوْنَ جَهَنَّمَ دَاخِرِيْنَ. بَارَكَ اللهُ لِيْ وَلَكُمْ فِي الْقُرْآنِ الْعَظِيْمِ. وَنَفَعَنِيْ وَإِيَّاكُمْ بِمَا فِيْهِ مِنَ الْآيَاتِ وَالذِّكْرِ الْحَكِيْمِ. أَسْتَغْفِرُ اللهَ لِيْ وَلَكُمْ وَلِسَائِرِ الْمُسْلِمِيْنَ. فَاسْتَغْفِرُوْهُ إِنَّهُ هُوَ الْغَفُوْرُ الرَّحِيْمُ.

The Second Khutbah — اَلْخُطْبَةُ الثَّانِيَةُ

اَلْحَمْدُ لِلهِ نَحْمَدُهُ وَنَسْتَعِيْنُهُ وَنَسْتَغْفِرُهُ وَنُؤْمِنُ بِهِ وَنَتَوَكَّلُ عَلَيْهِ. وَنَعُوْذُ بِاللهِ مِنْ شُرُوْرِ أَنْفُسِنَا وَمِنْ سَيِّئَاتِ أَعْمَالِنَا مَنْ يَهْدِهِ اللهُ فَلَا مُضِلَّ لَهُ مَنْ يُضْلِلْهُ فَلَا هَادِيَ لَهُ. وَنَشْهَدُ أَنْ لَا إِلَهَ إِلَّا اللهُ. وَنَشْهَدُ أَنَّ مُحَمَّدًا عَبْدُهُ وَرَسُوْلُهُ. **أَمَّا بَعْدُ.**

إِنَّ اللهَ وَمَلَائِكَتَهُ يُصَلُّوْنَ عَلَى النَّبِيِّ يَاأَيُّهَا الَّذِيْنَ آمَنُوْا صَلُّوْا عَلَيْهِ وَسَلِّمُوْا تَسْلِيْمًا. اَللَّهُمَّ صَلِّ عَلَى مُحَمَّدٍ بِعَدَدِ مَنْ صَلَّى وَصَامَ. اَللَّهُمَّ صَلِّ عَلَى مُحَمَّدٍ بِعَدَدِ مَنْ قَعَدَ وَقَامَ. وَصَلِّ عَلَى جَمِيْعِ الْأَنْبِيَاءِ وَالْمُرْسَلِيْنَ وَعَلَى مَلَائِكَتِهِ الْمُقَرَّبِيْنَ وَعَلَى عِبَادِ اللهِ الصَّالِحِيْنَ بِرَحْمَتِكَ يَا أَرْحَمَ الرَّاحِمِيْنَ.

عِبَادَ اللهِ رَحِمَكُمُ اللهُ. إِنَّ اللهَ يَأْمُرُ بِالْعَدْلِ وَالْإِحْسَانِ وَإِيْتَاءِ ذِي الْقُرْبَى وَيَنْهَى عَنِ الْفَحْشَاءِ وَالْمُنْكَرِ وَالْبَغْيِ. يَعِظُكُمْ لَعَلَّكُمْ تَذَكَّرُوْنَ فَاذْكُرُوْنِيْ أَذْكُرْكُمْ وَاشْكُرُوْا لِيْ وَلَا تَكْفُرُوْنِ. **أَقِيْمُوا الصَّلَاةَ.**

Sajdah Tilawat

Level 1

Definition: Sajdah Tilawat means to make a Sajdah after reading or hearing an Aayat of Sajdah from the Quran. There are 14 Aayaat of Sajdah in the Quran.

Status: Sajdah Tilaawat is Waajib (compulsory) for the one who reads the Sajdah Aayah as well as the one who heard it.

The Method of Sajdah Tilawat:

Out of Salaah: On reading the verse of Sajdah, a person should say *Allahu Akbar* (without raising the hands) and go into Sajdah. Recite the Tasbeeh in Sajdah three times and then come up from Sajdah. A person has the option of making the Sajdah from the standing posture or from the sitting posture.

In Salaah: As soon as the Sajdah verse is recited in Salaah, one should immediately make a Sajdah and then continue the Salaah as normal.

Note: The conditions that are a prerequisite for Salaah, are also a prerequisite for Sajdah Tilawat i.e. to have Wudhu, to face the Qiblah, to be clean, etc.

Level 2
The 14 Verses of Sajdah In the Quran

No.	Para	Surah	Verse No.	No.	Para	Surah	Verse No.
1.	9	7. Al-A'raf	206	8.	19	27. An-Naml	26
2.	13	13. Ar-Ra'd	15	9.	21	32. As-Sajdah	15
3.	14	16. Al-Nahl	50	10.	23	38. Swaad	24
4.	15	17. Al-Isra	109	11.	24	41. Fussilat	38
5.	16	19. Maryam	58	12.	27	53. An-Najm	62
6.	17	22. Al-Hajj	18	13.	30	84. Inshiqaq	21
7.	19	25. Al-Furqan	60	14.	30	96. Al-Alaq	19

Sajdah Sahw

Level 1

Definition: Sajdah Sahw are two Sajdahs made when one makes a mistake in Salaah.

Status: Sajdah Sahw is Waajib when an error is made in Salaah.

The Method of Sajdah Sahw:

In the last sitting (Qa'dah Akheerah) after reciting Tashahhud;

1. Make one Salaam to the right side.
2. Then make two Sajdahs.
3. Thereafter recite Tashahhud.
4. Recite Durood Ibraheem.
5. Recite the Dua after Durood.
6. Make Salaam on both sides.

Level 2

When does Sajdah Sahw become Waajib?

1. If any Waajibaat is missed out.
2. If any Waajibaat is delayed.
3. If the order of any Waajibaat is changed.
4. If any Fardh act is delayed.
5. If any Fardh act is performed before its time.
6. If any Fardh act is repeated.

Salaah of a Masbooq (Late-Comer)

Level 1

Definition: A Masbooq is a person who joins the Jamaat salaah after the Imaam has completed one or more Rakaats.

Rules of joining the Imaam after he has started the Salaah:

1. If you have joined in late for the Jamaat Salaah, do the following, say the Takbeer tahreemah, fold your hands, stand for a moment and then join the Imaam in whichever posture he is in. Do not recite Thana.
2. The Masbooq should join the Jamaat without any delay.
3. If a Masbooq joins the Jamaat before or whilst the Imaam is in Ruku, then he will not repeat that Rakat.
4. If a Masbooq joins the Jamaat after the Ruku e.g. in Qaumah or Sajdah, he will have to repeat that Rakat.
5. Once the Imaam makes the first Salaam, one cannot join the Jamaat.

The Method of completing missed Rakaats:

Note: The Masbooq should only stand up after the Imaam makes both Salaams. If a Masbooq has missed:

One Rakat: He should stand up after the Imaam's Salaam, read Thana, Ta'awwudh, Tasmiyah, Surah Fatiha, a Surah and complete the Salaah as normal.

Two Rakaats: He should stand up after the Imaam's Salaam, read Thana, Ta'awwudh, Tasmiyah, Surah Fatiha, a Surah and complete both the rakaats of the Salaah as usual. (The method will differ in Maghrib Salaah).

In the Maghrib Salaah: If a person missed two Rakaats, he should stand up after the Imaam's Salaam, read Thana, Ta'awwudh, Tasmiyah, Surah Fatiha, and a Surah. Thereafter he will perform Ruku and Sajdah, however after the second Sajdah he will sit for the first Qa'dah. Thereafter he will stand up for the third Rakat, read Surah Fatiha, a Surah and complete the Salaah as normal.

Three Rakaats: The Masbooq will stand up after the Imaam's Salaam, read Thana, Ta'awwudh, Tasmiyah, Surah Fatiha, a Surah and after the second Sajdah, he will sit for the first Qa'dah. Thereafter stand up and perform the second Rakat. In the second Rakat he will recite Tasmiyah, Surah Fatiha, and a Surah. Finally he will perform the third Rakat wherein he will only recite Surah Fatiha. No Surah will be recited. Complete the Salaah as normal.

Four Rakaats: Stand up after the Imaam's Salaam and perform four Rakaats as one would normally perform four Rakaats Salaah.

Salaah of a Musaafir (Traveler)

Level 1

Definition: A Musaafir is a person who travels more than 48 miles and does not intend to stay at his destination for more than 15 days.

Rules of Salaah of a Musaafir:
1. The Musaafir will perform Qasr (pray two Rakaats instead of four) **only** for the Fardh of Dhuhr, 'Asr, and 'Ishaa. He will pray all other Salaahs as normal.
2. If the Musaafir is praying behind an Imaam, he will follow the Imaam and complete four Rakaats.
3. If the Musaafir is Imaam, he will pray his two Rakaats and then inform the followers to complete their remaining Rakaats.

The Messenger of Allah ﷺ said:
"When you leave your house, perform two Rakaats and this will safeguard you against evil. When you enter your home, perform another two Rakaats and this will safeguard you against evil."
[Musnad Al-Bazzar]

Salaah of a Mareedh (Sick)

Level 1

Definition: A Mareedh is a person who is so ill that he is unable to pray Salaah normally.

Rules of Salaah of a Mareedh:

1. If a person is unable to stand up, or standing up will increase his illness, or he is unable to stand up but unable to go to Ruku or Sajdah, then he will pray sitting down.
2. If he is praying while sitting and he is unable to make Ruku and Sajdah, then he will make Ruku and Sajdah by bowing his head and he should bow more for Sajdah.
3. If a person is unable to sit, then he should lie on his back with heads and knees raised and his head and feet facing the Qiblah. Then he will make Ruku and Sajdah through gestures.
4. If a person is unable to raise his knees, then he can stretch his legs towards the Qiblah and if he is unable to lie on his back, he can lie down on his sides with his head towards the Qiblah. It is more preferable to lie on his right side.

Dua for the Sick

اَللّٰهُمَّ رَبَّ النَّاسِ ، مُذْهِبَ الْبَأْسِ اِشْفِ أَنْتَ الشَّافِيْ ، لَا شَافِيَ إِلَّا أَنْتَ ، شِفَاءٌ لَا يُغَادِرُ سَقَمًا

Allaahumma rabbannaas mudh hibal ba-si ishfi antash shaafee laa shaafia illaa anta shifaa-un laa ughaadiru saqaman

O Allah, the Lord of the people! Remove the trouble and heal the patient, for You are the Healer. No healing is of any avail but Yours; healing that will leave behind no ailment.

Eid Salaah

Level 1

Definition: Eid Salaah is performed on the days of Eid-ul-Fitr and Eid-ul-Adha with six extra Takbeers.

Status: Waajib (compulsory)

Level 2

The Method of Eid Salaah:

1. Make Niyyah as follows: "I am performing two Rakaats Eid-ul-Fitr or Eid-ul-Adha with six extra Takbeers."
2. After Takbeer Tahreemah, fold the hands and recite the Thana as normal.
3. Thereafter raise both the hands up to the ears and while saying اللهُ أَكْبَر bring them down to the sides. This is the first extra Takbeer.
4. Do the same (as explained in no. 3) for the second extra Takbeer.
5. For the third extra Takbeer, once again raise the hands to the ears, then while saying lower them and tie them below the navel.
6. Thereafter complete the first Rakat as normal.
7. In the second Rakat, after reciting the Qiraat (before going into Ruku) raise the hands to the ears and make three Takbeers. This will be the fourth, fifth, and sixth extra Takbeer. For each Takbeer raise both hands up to the ears and while saying bring them down to the side.
8. Then say a fourth Takbeer without raising the hands and go into Ruku.
9. The Salaah will thereafter continue as normal.
10. After the Eid Salaah, the Imaam will first make dua and thereafter deliver the two Khutbahs. It is Waajib to listen to both the Khutbahs after the Eid Salaah.

Sunan of the Day of Eid:

1. Cleanse your mouth using the Miswaak.
2. Take a Ghusl.
3. Dress in your best clothing (i.e. the best clothing in your possession, not necessarily new clothing).
4. Apply 'Itr (perfume).
5. Perform Eid Salaah at the Eid Gaah (i.e. open field).
6. Avoid eating anything before Eid Salaah on the day of Eid-ul-Adha (i.e. the first thing one should consume should be the meat of the sacrificed animal). However, on the day of Eid-ul-Fitr, you should eat an odd number of dates or anything sweet before leaving for the Eid Salaah.
7. Go to the Eid Gaah early.
8. Walk to the place of Eid Salaah.
9. Recite the Takbeer audibly when proceeding to the Eid Gaah on the day of Eid-ul-Adha, and recite the Takbeer silently when proceeding for the Eid Salaah on the day of Eid-ul-Fitr. After reaching the Eid Gaah, continue reciting the Takbeer until the Imaam comes out to conduct the Eid.
10. Use different routes to and from the place of Eid Salaah.
11. Perform two Rakaats Waajib Salaah of Eid with six extra Takbeers without any Adhaan or Iqaamah.
12. Remain seated after the Eid Salaah and listen to the Khutbah.
13. During the Khutbah, it is Waajib for one to remain silent and listen attentively to the Khutbah.
14. It is forbidden to perform any Nafl Salaah in the Eid Gaah, both before and after the Eid Salaah.
15. By staying awake and engaging in Ibaadah on the night of Eid, one will be rewarded in this manner that when all the hearts die, his heart will remain alive.

Janaazah Salaah

Level 1

Definition: Janaazah Salaah is a Dua (supplication) for the Mayyit (deceased Muslim) before they are buried.

Status: Fardh Kifaayah.

2 Faraaidh of Janaazah Salaah:
1. Qiyaam (to stand for the Salaah.)   2. To recite four Takbeers.

Level 2

The Method of Janaazah Salaah:
1. The body of the Mayyit (the deceased) should be placed in front of the Imaam, with the head of the Mayyit on the right hand side of the Imaam.
2. The Imaam should stand in line with the chest of the Mayyit.
3. It is Mustahabb to make an odd number of Saffs (rows). The Saffs should be close to one another as there is no Ruku and Sajdah to be made.
4. Make Niyyah: "I am performing this Janaazah Salaah for the sake of Allah Ta'ala."
5. The Imaam will **raise** his hands up to his ears and say the Takbeer loudly. The Muqtadees (followers) should also raise their hands and say the Takbeer SOFTLY. Then they should tie the hands below the navel as normally done.
6. Thereafter recite the Thana of Janaazah Salaah SOFTLY.
7. The Imaam will then say the Takbeer aloud and the Muqtadees (followers) SOFTLY for the second time. The hands should **not** be raised when saying this Takbeer and for the remaining Takbeers.
8. After the second Takbeer, recite Durood Ibraheem.
9. Thereafter the third Takbeer should be said in the same manner. Then Duaas should be recited based on the Mayyit.
10. The Imaam will then say the 4th Takbeer and make Salaam to the right and left. The Muqtadees should follow by saying the Takbeer and Salaam SOFTLY.

Duaas of Janaazah Salaah

Level 1

1. Thana in Janaazah Salaah

سُبْحَانَكَ اللّٰهُمَّ وَبِحَمْدِكَ ، وَتَبَارَكَ اسْمُكَ ، وَتَعَالٰى جَدُّكَ ، وَجَلَّ ثَنَاؤُكَ ، وَلَا إِلٰهَ غَيْرُكَ

Subhaanaka Allaahumma wabi hamdika watabaara kasmuka wata'aalaa jadduka wa jalla thanaa-uka walaa ilaaha ghayruka.

O Allah, glorified are You and praise be to You. Blessed is Your name, and exalted is Your majesty and elevated is Your praise. There is no one worthy of worship but You.

Level 2

2. Dua in Janaazah Salaah for an adult

اَللّٰهُمَّ اغْفِرْ لِحَيِّنَا وَمَيِّتِنَا وَشَاهِدِنَا وَغَائِبِنَا وَصَغِيرِنَا وَكَبِيرِنَا وَذَكَرِنَا وَأُنْثَانَا ، اَللّٰهُمَّ مَنْ أَحْيَيْتَهُ مِنَّا فَأَحْيِهِ عَلَى الْإِسْلَامِ ، وَمَنْ تَوَفَّيْتَهُ مِنَّا فَتَوَفَّهُ عَلَى الْإِيْمَانِ

Allaahummaghfir lihayyinaa wa mayyitinaa wa shaahidinaa wa ghaa-ibinaa wa sagheerinaa wa kabeerinaa wa dhakarinaa wa unthaanaa
Allaahumma man ahyaytahu minnaa fa ahyihee 'alal islam wa man tawaffaytahu minnaa fatawaffahu 'alal eemaan

O Allah, forgive our people who are still alive and who passed away, those who are present here and those absent, forgive our young and our old, and our males and females. O Allah, the one whom You wish to keep alive, make him live according to Islam and the one whom You wish to take their life, then grant him death with Imaan.

3. Janaazah Dua for a young boy

اَللّٰهُمَّ اجْعَلْهُ لَنَا فَرَطًا ، وَاجْعَلْهُ لَنَا أَجْرًا وَذُخْرًا ، وَاجْعَلْهُ لَنَا شَافِعًا وَمُشَفَّعًا

Allaahummaj'alhu lanaa farataw waj'alhu lanaa ajraw wa dhukhraw waj'alhu lanaa shaafi'aw wa mushaffa'aa

O Allah, make him a means of salvation for us and make him a reward and treasure for us and an intercessor whose intercession is accepted.

4. Janaazah Dua for a young girl

اَللّٰهُمَّ اجْعَلْهَا لَنَا فَرَطًا ، وَاجْعَلْهَا لَنَا أَجْرًا وَذُخْرًا ، وَاجْعَلْهَا لَنَا شَافِعَةً وَمُشَفَّعَةً

Allaahummaj'alhaa lanaa farataw waj'alhaa lanaa ajraw wa dhukhraw waj'alhaa lanaa shaafi'ataw wa mushaffa'ah

O Allah, make her a means of salvation for us and make her a reward and treasure for us and an intercessor whose intercession is accepted.

مَنِ اتَّبَعَ جَنَازَةَ مُسْلِمٍ إِيمَانًا وَاحْتِسَابًا، وَكَانَ مَعَهُ حَتَّى يُصَلَّيَ عَلَيْهَا، وَيَفْرُغَ مِنْ دَفْنِهَا، فَإِنَّهُ يَرْجِعُ مِنَ الْأَجْرِ بِقِيرَاطَيْنِ، كُلُّ قِيرَاطٍ مِثْلُ أُحُدٍ، وَمَنْ صَلَّى عَلَيْهَا ثُمَّ رَجَعَ قَبْلَ أَنْ تُدْفَنَ فَإِنَّهُ يَرْجِعُ بِقِيرَاطٍ

The Messenger of Allah ﷺ said: "(A believer) who accompanies the funeral procession of a Muslim out of sincere faith and hoping to attain Allah's reward and remains with it till the funeral prayer is offered and the burial ceremonies are over, he will return with a reward of two Qirats. Each Qirat is like the size of the (Mount) Uhud. He who offers the funeral prayer only and returns before the burial, will return with the reward of one Qirat only." [Bukhaari]

Zakaah

Level 1

Definition: Zakaah is to give 1/40th or 2.5% of one's wealth to the poor and needy Muslims once a year.

Status: It is Fardh (obligatory) to give Zakaah for the one who owns the required amount of wealth (Nisaab) once a year.

Zakaah is Fardh on:
1. The one who is muslim.
2. The one who is baaligh (reached puberty).
3. The one who is sane.
4. The one who is free.
5. The one who owns the required amount of wealth (Nisaab):
    a. Fully owned by him for one complete lunar year.
    b. Extra from his personal needs (clothing, furniture, car, etc)
    c. Gives profit or benefit (gold, silver, livestock, merchandise of business)

Types of wealth Zakaah is Fardh on:
1. Zakaah is Fardh on gold and silver, whether they are in the form of jewelry, cash, or any other form. The Nisaab of gold is 87.48 grams and the nisaab of silver is 612.36 grams.
    a. Zakaah is not Fardh on any other metal nor precious gemstones.
    b. Zakaah is not Fardh on imitation jewelry.
2. Zakaah is Fardh on business merchandise equivalent to the value of Nisaab.
    a. Zakaah is Fardh on income from properties and hiring businesses.
3. Zakaah is Fardh on livestock.
    a. Zakaah is not Fardh on horses, donkeys, and mules that are not for trade.

Level 2

Avenues of Zakaah:

1. Zakaah can be given to a needy person or a person who does not own Nisaab.
2. Zakaah can be given to a slave that has a contract with his master to buy his freedom.
3. Zakaah can be given to the one who is in debt and does not own any wealth to repay it.
4. Zakaah can be given to the one who is in the path of Allah and is in need of wealth to complete their duty.
5. Zakaah can be given to the one who is traveling and runs out of wealth/basic necessities needed to return home.
6. Zakaah can be given to one's relatives as long as they fit within one of the above categories but Zakaah cannot be given to one's parents, grandparents, children, grandchildren, and spouse even if they are from the above groups.
7. Zakaah cannot be given to any non Muslim.
8. Zakaah cannot be given to Banu Haashim. They are the relatives of Muhammed ﷺ and their descendants.
9. Zakaah cannot be given to institutes or organizations for the sake of their constructions, investments, and salaries.
10. Zakaah cannot be given to assist the burial of a dead Muslim.

مَا نَقَصَتْ صَدَقَةٌ مِنْ مَالٍ وَمَا زَادَ اللهُ عَبْدًا بِعَفْوٍ إِلَّا عِزًّا وَمَا تَوَاضَعَ أَحَدٌ لِلهِ إِلَّا رَفَعَهُ اللهُ

The Messenger of Allah ﷺ said:
"Charity does not decrease wealth, no one forgives another except that Allah increases his honor, and no one humbles himself for the sake of Allah except that Allah raises his status." [Muslim]

Sawm

Level 1

Definition: Sawm is to stay away from eating and drinking from Fajr till Maghrib during the month of Ramadhan.

Status: Fardh (obligatory)

Faraaidh of Sawm:
1. To have Niyyah (Intention) of fasting by midday.
2. To stay away from everything that breaks the fast.

Sunan of Sawm:
1. To eat Sehri.
2. To break the fast immediately after sunset.
3. To perform Taraweeh Salaah at night.
4. To feed the poor and hungry.
5. To increase the reading of the Quran.
6. To observe I'tikaaf in the Masjid during the last ten days of Ramadhan.

Mustahabbaat of Sawm:
1. To delay the Sehri till a little while before Fajr.
2. To break one's fast with dates and if dates are not available, then water.
3. To make Niyyah (intention) the night before.

The Messenger of Allah ﷺ said: *"There has come to you Ramadhan, a blessed month, which Allah, the Mighty and Sublime, has enjoined you to fast. In it the gates of heavens are opened and the gates of Hell are closed, and every devil is chained up. In it Allah has a night which is better than a thousand months; whoever is deprived of its goodness is indeed deprived."* [Nasai]

Level 2
Makroohaat of Sawm:
1. To chew plastic, rubber, or any such items.
2. To taste any food and drink, then to spit it out.
3. To collect saliva in the mouth and to swallow it.
4. To delay a Fardh Ghusl knowingly after Fajr.
5. To use toothpaste or tooth powder.
6. To complain of hunger and thirst.
7. To take the water too much up the nose when washing it.
8. To gargle more than necessary.
9. To argue or to use indecent words
10. To backbite, lie, curse, and other sins will be more severe.

Level 3
Mufsidaat of Sawm:
1. Qadha will be necessary if anything was put by force into the mouth.
2. Qadha will be necessary if one swallows something that was stuck between the teeth if it was bigger than a grain.
    - Qadha will not be necessary if it was smaller than a grain.
    - Qadha will be necessary if he removes it then swallows it, regardless of its size.
3. Qadha will be necessary if one vomits a mouthful intentionally or returns vomit down the throat.
    - Qadha will not be necessary if one vomits a mouthful unintentionally.
4. Qadha will be necessary if swallowing items that are not food or medicine intentionally like pebbles, paper, etc.
    - Qadha will not be necessary if a fly, mosquito, or any other object goes down his throat unintentionally.
5. Qadha will be necessary if oil goes into the ear.
    - Qadha will not be necessary if water goes into the ear.
6. Qadha will be necessary if snuff is inhaled into the nose.

7. Qadha will be necessary if one swallows blood that is more than his saliva.
    - Qadha will not be necessary if one swallows his own saliva.
8. Qadha will be necessary if one eats and drinks forgetfully and then continues to eat and drink thinking that his fast is broken.
    - Qadha will not be necessary if one eats and drinks forgetfully and then continues to keep his fast after he remembers.
9. Qadha will be necessary if one eats or drinks mistakenly (while he remembers that he is fasting) like water going down the throat when gargling.
    - Qadha will not be necessary if dust or dirt goes down the throat.
10. Qadha will be necessary if one eats or drinks after Fajr or before sunset due to cloudy weather or a faulty clock and then realizing one's mistake.
11. Qadha and Kaffarah will be necessary if one eats, drinks, or breaks the fast in any way without a valid reason.
    - Kaffarah means to fast for 60 days <u>consecutively.</u> If he is unable to do that, then he must feed 60 poor people two meals or give each of them the value of 3 ½ lbs of wheat.
12. Qadha and Kaffarah will be necessary if one applies surma on his eyes or oil on his head and then continues to eat and drink thinking that his fast is broken.
    - Qadha will not be necessary if one applies surma on his eyes, contact lenses, or oil on his head or body by itself.
13. Qadha and Kaffarah will be necessary if one drinks any medicine intentionally without a valid excuse. This includes an asthma pump, a nebulizer, and nose drops.
    - Qadha will not be necessary if one takes an injection, eye drops, or ear drops, or takes a blood test.

The Messenger of Allah ﷺ said: ***"The five daily prayers, Jumu'ah to Jumu'ah, and Ramadhan to Ramadhan expiate for (the sins perpetrated) in between them, so long as one stays away from the major sins."*** [Muslim]

Duaas of Sawm

1. Dua at the approach of Ramadhan

اَللّٰهُمَّ سَلِّمْنِيْ لِرَمَضَانَ ، وَسَلِّمْ رَمَضَانَ لِيْ ، وَسَلِّمْهُ لِيْ مُتَقَبَّلًا

Allaahumma sallimnee liramadhaana wa sallim ramdhaana lee wa sallimhu lee mutaqabbalaa

O Allah! Safeguard me for the month of Ramadhan and safeguard the month of Ramadhan for me and accept it from me.

2. Dua when breaking fast

اَللّٰهُمَّ لَكَ صُمْتُ ، وَعَلٰى رِزْقِكَ أَفْطَرْتُ

Allaahumma laka swumtu wa 'ala rizqika aftwartu

O Allah! For You I have fasted and upon Your provision, I have broken my fast.

3. Dua after Iftar

ذَهَبَ الظَّمَأُ ، وَابْتَلَّتِ الْعُرُوقُ ، وَثَبَتَ الْأَجْرُ إِنْ شَاءَ اللهُ

Dhahabaz zhama-u wabb tallatil 'urooq wa thabatal ajru in shaa Allaah

Thirst is gone, the veins are moistened, and the reward is certain if Allah wills.

4. Dua during Laylatul Qadr

اَللّٰهُمَّ إِنَّكَ عَفُوٌّ كَرِيْمٌ ، تُحِبُّ الْعَفْوَ ، فَاعْفُ عَنِّيْ

Allaahumma innaka Afuwwun kareemun tuhibbul 'afwa fa'fu 'annee

O Allah, indeed You are Pardoning and Generous. You love to pardon, so pardon me.

Level 2

5. Alternative Duaas for Iftar

اَلْحَمْدُ لِلهِ أَعَانَنِيْ فَصُمْتُ ، وَرَزَقَنِيْ فَأَفْطَرْتُ

Alhamdulillaahu a'aananee faswumtu warazaqanee fa-aftwartu

All praise is due to Allah who assisted me so I fasted and who provided for me so I could complete my fast.

اَللّٰهُمَّ لَكَ صُمْنَا ، وَعَلٰى رِزْقِكَ أَفْطَرْنَا ، فَتَقَبَّلْ مِنَّا ، إِنَّكَ أَنْتَ السَّمِيْعُ الْعَلِيْمُ

Allaahumma laka swumnaa wa 'ala rizqika aftwarnaa fataqabbal minnaa innaka intas samee'ul 'aleem

O Allah! For You we have fasted and upon Your provision, we have broken our fast. So accept from us. Indeed, You are the All-Hearing, All-Knowing.

اَللّٰهُمَّ إِنِّيْ أَسْأَلُكَ بِرَحْمَتِكَ الَّتِيْ وَسِعَتْ كُلَّ شَيْءٍ أَنْ تَغْفِرَ لِيْ

Allaahumma inner as-aluka birahmatikal latee wasi'at kulla shay-in an taghfira lee

O Allah, I ask You by Your mercy which envelops all things, that You forgive me.

يَا وَاسِعَ الْمَغْفِرَةِ ، اِغْفِرْ لِيْ

Yaa waasi'al maghfirah ighfir lee

O the One of abundant forgiveness! Forgive me.

I'tikaaf

Level 1

Definition: I'tikaaf is to enter the Masjid with the intention of staying in the Masjid.

Status: It is Sunnah Mu'akkadah Kifaayah to stay in the Masjid (without leaving) during the last ten days and ten nights of Ramadhan.

Conditions of I'tikaaf:

1. The one who is muslim.
2. The one who is a male.
    - The I'tikaaf of a female is in her house.
3. The one who is sane.
4. The one who is pure (does not have to do Fardh Ghusl).
5. Niyyah (intention).

Level 2

Permissible actions of I'tikaaf:

1. It is permissible to eat and sleep in the Masjid.
2. It is permissible to discuss matters of Deen or <u>necessary</u> talks.
    - It is recommended that one remains engaged in Ibaadah like performing Nafl Salaah, reciting Quran and Dhikr, and learning the knowledge of Deen.
3. It is permissible to leave the Masjid for Fardh Ghusl.
4. It is permissible to leave the Masjid for Wudhu.
5. It is permissible to leave the Masjid to use the bathroom.
    - To leave without a valid reason will nullify the I'tikaaf.

Sadaqatul Fitr

Level 1

Definition: Sadaqatul Fitr is an extra charity a person must give on the day of Eid-ul-Fitr.

Status: Waajib (compulsory)

Level 2

Sadaqatul Fitr is Fardh on:
1. The one who is muslim.
   - The guardian should pay Sadaqatul Fitr on behalf of his immature or insane children born before the day.
2. The one who is free.
3. The one who owns the Nisaab of Zakaah.
   - The Nisaab does not have to be held for one complete lunar year unlike Zakaah.

Level 3

Rulings of Sadaqatul Fitr:
1. The time of Sadaqatul Fitr starts from after Fajr Salaah on the Day of Eid-ul-Fitr.
2. It should be given before one reaches the Eid Gaah, but it can be given after the Salaah.
3. It can also be given before the day of Eid, during the month of Ramadhan, and if not given on the day of Eid, must still be given afterwards.
4. Sadaqatul Fitr is to give 4.2 lbs of wheat, flour, or raisins or 8.4 lbs of dates or barley or their equivalent value.
5. The avenues of Sadaqatul Fitr are the same as the avenues of Zakaah.

Taraweeh Salaah
Level 1

Definition: Taraweeh Salaah is an extra Salaah a person performs during the nights of Ramadhan.

Status: It is Sunnah Mu'akkadah for male and female to perform Taraweeh Salaah. It is Sunnah Kifaayah for males to perform Taraweeh Salaah with Jamaat.

Level 2

Rulings of Taraweeh:

1. Taraweeh Salaah is 20 Rakaats with 10 Salaams. One must make Niyyah of two Rakaats each time.
2. It is Mustahabb to rest awhile after every four Rakaats. One can recite Quran quietly or pray Nafl Salaah during this period.
3. The time for Taraweeh Salaah is from after 'Ishaa till a little before Fajr time and can be performed before or after Witr Salaah.
4. It is Makrooh to perform Taraweeh Salaah sitting down if one has the strength to stand up.
5. It is Makrooh to join later when the Imaam is about to go to Ruku.

The Purpose of Fasting

يَا أَيُّهَا الَّذِيْنَ آمَنُوْا كُتِبَ عَلَيْكُمُ الصِّيَامُ كَمَا كُتِبَ عَلَى الَّذِيْنَ مِنْ قَبْلِكُمْ لَعَلَّكُمْ تَتَّقُوْنَ

"Fasting is prescribed for you, as it was prescribed for those before you, so that you may attain Taqwaa (piety and mindfulness of Allah)." (2:183)

Hajj

Level 1

Definition: Hajj is to visit the sacred house of Allah during the Days of Hajj (8-12 of Dhul-Hijjah) at least once in a person's life.

Status: It is Fardh (obligatory) to perform Hajj once in a lifetime.

Hajj is Fardh on:
1. The one who is muslim.
2. The one who is baaligh (reached puberty).
3. The one who is sane.
4. The one who is free.
5. The one who is financially independent to travel and has left sufficient provisions behind for one's dependents during their absence.
6. Security of Route.
7. A woman must be accompanied by her husband or Mahram.

3 Types of Hajj:
1. Qiraan: To perform 'Umrah (in the months of Hajj), then Hajj with **one** Ihraam.
2. Tamattu': To perform 'Umrah first with one Ihraam, then Hajj with a new Ihraam.
3. Ifraad: To perform Hajj only.

3 Faraaidh of Hajj:
1. Ihraam with Niyyah and Talbiyah.
2. Wuqoof at 'Arafah.
3. Tawaaf of Ziyaarah.

Level 2

6 Waajibaat of Hajj:

1. Wuqoof at Muzdalifah.
2. Rami: Pelting the Jamaraat (three stone pillars).
3. Nahr: Animal Sacrifice.
4. Halq or Qasr: Shaving or Trimming the Head.
5. Sa'ee between Safa and Marwa.
6. Tawaaf of Wada': Farewell Tawaaf.

Rulings of Ihraam:

1. Before reaching the Meeqaat (boundary) the person should perform Ghusl if possible, if not then Wudhu. The men will then put on the clothes of Ihraam, two (preferably white) unstitched sheets, and put on 'Itr and women will remain in their normal clothes.

2. Then they should perform two Rakaats Salaat of Ihraam and read Surah Kafiroon in the first Rakat and Surah Ikhlas in the second.

3. Then they will make an intention and read the Talbiyah (men will always read Talbiyah loudly while women will read silently) and they will now be in the state of Ihraam.

4. In the state of Ihraam it is impermissible to have any relations with one's spouse.

5. In the state of Ihraam it is impermissible to hunt and kill any animals (even lice) or even help or guide anyone to hunt.

6. In the state of Ihraam it is impermissible to use any perfume, 'Itr, or anything that has a scent (toothpaste) on the clothes or body.
    - In the state of Ihraam it is permissible to use Miswaak.

7. In the state of Ihraam it is impermissible to remove any hair or trim any nail.

8. In the state of Ihraam it is impermissible for men to wear stitched clothing.

    ○ In the state of Ihraam it is permissible to wear a ring, a pair of glasses, a wristwatch, and a belt that holds one's money.

9. In the state of Ihraam it is impermissible for men to wear any footwear that covers the central bone on the top of their feet.

10. In the state of Ihraam it is impermissible for men to cover their head and face.

    ○ In the state of Ihraam it is permissible to carry something on the head.

11. In the state of Ihraam it is impermissible for women to wear a covering that touches their face. They should cover their face in such a way that it does not touch their face.

12. In the state of Ihraam it is impermissible to harm anyone, physically or verbally, argue, and use indecent and foul language.

Level 3

Method of Hajj:

1. They should enter the state of Ihraam before the 8th of Dhul-Hijjah. To enter Ihraam a person must wear the clothes of Ihraam (with males leaving their head uncovered), then pray two Rakaats Salaat of Ihraam, then he must make Niyyah and read the Talbiyah.

2. Those that intended Qiraan will complete his 'Umrah and stay in Ihraam. Those that intended Tamattu' will complete his 'Umrah and leave Ihraam by shaving/trimming his head, then he will enter into a new Ihraam.

3. They will do Tawaaf of Qudoom when they reach Makkah and pray two Rakaats of Salaat of Tawaaf afterwards. (It is better for a person doing Qiraan to do Sa'ee after this Tawaaf, instead of Tawaaf of Ziyaarah.)

4. Before Dhuhr of the 8th of Dhul-Hijjah they should be at Mina until Fajr of the following day. Do as much Ibaadah as possible.

5. After Sunrise of the 9th of Dhul-Hijjah, they should leave for 'Arafah and spend time there. They should try to do as much extra Ibaadah as they can near Jabal Rahmah.

6. With the Imaam of 'Arafah they will read Dhuhr and 'Asr Salaah together in congregation.

7. After sunset they will go to Muzdalifah and with the Imaam of Muzdalifah, they will read Maghrib and 'Ishaa Salaat together in the time of 'Ishaa. (Stones should also be collected here for the following days.)

8. After Fajr of the 10th of Dhul-Hijjah, they will go back to Mina and perform Rami (pelt the largest of the three Jamaraat) with 7 stones.

9. Then they will sacrifice their animal and shave/trim their hair after that.

10. Then they must return to Makkah to perform Tawaaf of Ziyaarah. They have until sunset on the 12th of Dhul-Hijjah. Men will do Raml (move briskly) in the first three rounds and Idhtibaa (uncover the right shoulder) in all rounds. All restrictions of Ihraam will be removed after this Tawaaf.

11. Afterwards, they will pray two Rakaats Salaat of Tawaaf near Maqaam Ibraheem and perform Sa'ee. Men will run between the two green lights.

12. On the 11th and 12th, they will return to Mina and pelt all three Jamaraat with 7 stones each. (If a person does not leave before sunset on the 12th, they will have to pelt them on the 13th as well.)

13. Before returning home, they will perform one last Tawaaf, known as the Farewell Tawaaf, and pray two Rakaats Salaat of Tawaaf afterwards.

Qurbani

Level 1

Definition: Qurbani is to sacrifice an animal on Eid-ul-Adha for the one who is not in Hajj.

Status: Waajib (compulsory)

Qurbani is Waajib on:
1. The one who is muslim.
2. The one who is baaligh (reached puberty).
3. The one who is sane.
4. The one who is free.
5. The one who owns the Nisaab of Zakaah.
   - But the Nisaab does not have to be held for one complete lunar year.

Level 2

Rulings of Qurbani:

1. The time of Qurbani starts from after Eid Salaah on the 10th of Dhul-Hijjah till the sunset of the 12th of Dhul-Hijjah. It is better to do Qurbani as early as possible. This timing is for the one living in a town.

2. The time of Qurbani for the one living in a village starts from after Fajr on the Day of Eid. Similarly, if the one who lives in a town sends his animal to be slaughtered in the village, then his animal can be slaughtered before Eid Salaah.

3. It is Mustahabb for those that are intending Qurbani to not cut any hair or to clip their nails from the beginning of Dhul-Hijjah till after the Qurbani.

4. If an animal bought for Qurbani was not slaughtered in the days of slaughter, then it must be given away alive as charity.

5. The Qurbani can be made from goats and sheep by one share only and from cows and camels by seven shares. The animals can be male or female, but they should be healthy and free from defects.

6. Goats and sheeps must be at least one year old, the cow must be at least two and the camel must be at least five years old.

7. It is necessary for everyone to have the Niyyah of Qurbani. If anyone has any other intention, then the Qurbani will not be valid for any of the shareholders.

8. It is permissible for the person to eat the meat himself or to give the meat to whoever he wishes, but it is Mustahabb to divide the meat into three parts; 1) for home, 2) for relatives, 3) for the poor and needy.

Level 3

Method of Qurbani:

1. It is Mustahabb for the person to slaughter the animal themselves, if they are able, otherwise it is Mustahabb to be present while another Muslim slaughters it.

2. It is Mustahabb to sharpen the knife beforehand away from the animal and to not slaughter an animal in the presence of another animal.

3. It is Mustahabb to face the Qiblah while slaughtering.

4. He should lay the throat of the animal towards the Qiblah and recite the Dua.

5. It is necessary for at least *three* of the four veins in the throat to be cut, while reciting *Bismillaahi Allaahu Akbar*, like normal slaughtering.

6. He should then wait for the animal to turn completely cold before cutting and skinning the animal.

'Umrah

Level 1

Definition: 'Umrah is to visit the sacred house of Allah for Tawaaf and Sa'ee and can be done anytime of the year.

Status: It is Sunnah Mu'akkadah to perform 'Umrah once in a lifetime.

2 Faraaidh of 'Umrah:

1. Ihraam with Niyyah and Talbiyah.
2. At least four rounds of Tawaaf with its Niyyah.

3 Waajibaat of 'Umrah:

1. To complete the full Tawaaf with the two Rakaats Salaat of Tawaaf.
2. Sa'ee between Safa and Marwa.
3. Halq or Qasr: Shaving or Trimming the Head.

Level 2

Method of 'Umrah:

1. They should enter the state of Ihraam before the Meeqaat. To enter Ihraam a person must wear the clothes of Ihraam (with males leaving their head uncovered), then pray two Rakaats Salaat of Ihraam, then he must make Niyyah and read the Talbiyah.
2. For Tawaaf, Wudhu is required. Before beginning, they should stand in front of the Hajar Aswad to make Niyyah, Takbeer, and Istilaam.
3. Then they will start moving counterclockwise around the Ka'bah 7 times to complete the Tawaaf. During Tawaaf one should not face the chest (except for Istilaam of Hajar Aswad which he will do at the end of every round) or turn his back towards the Ka'bah.
4. Men will do Raml the first three rounds and do Idhtibaa for all rounds.

5. Then they will pray two Rakaats Salaat of Tawaaf near Maqaam Ibraheem and make Dua and drink Zamzam.
6. Before going to Sa'ee, they should Istilaam again for the 9th time.
7. When they reach Safa they will make dua, while facing the Ka'bah. At every hill, one should pause and make dua while facing the Ka'bah.
8. They will then complete the seven rounds of Sa'ee between Safa and Marwa. The men will run between the green lights every round.
9. Then the men will shave/trim their head while women will only trim a little from their hair. If the person is bald, they will pass a razor over their head.
10. The 'Umrah is complete and all restrictions of Ihraam have been removed.

Duaas of Hajj & 'Umrah

Level 1

1. Talbiyah

لَبَّيْكَ اَللَّهُمَّ لَبَّيْكَ ، لَبَّيْكَ لَا شَرِيْكَ لَكَ لَبَّيْكَ ، إِنَّ الْحَمْدَ وَالنِّعْمَةَ لَكَ وَالْمُلْكَ ، لَا شَرِيْكَ لَكَ

Labbayk Allaahumma labbayk, labbayka laa shareeka laka labbayk, innal hamda wanni'mata, laka wal mulk, laa shareeka laka

Ever at Your service, O Allah, every at Your service. Ever at Your Service, You have no partner, ever at Your service. Verily all praise, blessings and dominions are Yours. You have no partner.

2. Istilaam

بِسْمِ اللهِ ، اللهُ أَكْبَرُ وَلِلَّهِ الْحَمْدُ ، لَا إِلَهَ إِلَّا اللهُ ، وَالصَّلَاةُ وَالسَّلَامُ عَلَى رَسُوْلِ اللهِ

Bismillaahi Allaahu akbar wa lillaahil hamdu laa ilaaha illallaahu was swalaatu was salaamu 'alaa rasoolillaah

In the Name of Allah. Allah is the greatest and for Him is all praise and there is none worthy of worship besides Him. And salutations and peace be upon the Messenger of Allah.

3. Dua when drinking Zamzam

اَللّٰهُمَّ إِنِّيْ أَسْأَلُكَ عِلْمًا نَافِعًا ، وَرِزْقًا وَاسِعًا ، وَشِفَاءً مِنْ كُلِّ دَاءٍ

Allaahumma Innee As-aluka 'Ilmann Naafi'an wa Rizqan waasi'an wa shifaa-an min kulli daa

O Allah, I seek beneficial knowledge, wide sustenance, and cure from all ailments from You.

Level 2

4. Dua of Sa'ee

أَبْدَأُ بِمَا بَدَأَ اللّٰهُ بِهِ "إِنَّ الصَّفَا وَالْمَرْوَةَ مِنْ شَعَائِرِ اللّٰهِ" لَا إِلٰهَ إِلَّا اللّٰهُ وَاللّٰهُ أَكْبَرُ ، لَا إِلٰهَ إِلَّا اللّٰهُ وَحْدَهُ لَا شَرِيْكَ لَهُ ، لَهُ الْمُلْكُ وَلَهُ الْحَمْدُ ، وَهُوَ عَلَى كُلِّ شَيْءٍ قَدِيْرٌ ، لَا إِلٰهَ إِلَّا اللّٰهُ وَحْدَهُ ، أَنْجَزَ وَعْدَهُ ، وَنَصَرَ عَبْدَهُ ، وَهَزَمَ الْأَحْزَابَ وَحْدَهُ

Abda-u bimaa bada-allaahu bih Innas swafaa wal marwata min sha'aa-irillaah Laa-ilaaha illallaahu wahdahuu laa shareeka lahuu lahul mulku wa lahul hamdu wahuwa 'alaa kulli shai-inn qadeer, laa ilaaha illallaahu wahdahu, anjaza wa'dahu, wa naswara 'abdahu, wa hazamal ahzaaba wahdah

I begin with what Allah began with. Indeed, as-Safa and al-Marwah are among the symbols of Allah. There is none worthy of worship but Allah and Allah is the greatest. There is none worthy of worship but Allah, who is alone and has no partner. For Him is the kingdom and for Him is all praise. He has power over everything. None has the right to be worshiped except Allah alone. He fulfilled His promise, aided His Servant, and single-handedly defeated the confederates.

The Messenger of Allah ﷺ said: *"Perform Hajj and 'Umrah consecutively; for they remove poverty and sin as the bellows removes impurity from iron."*

[Nasai]

5. Dua when running between the green lights

رَبِّ اغْفِرْ وَارْحَمْ ، إِنَّكَ أَنْتَ الْأَعَزُّ الْأَكْرَمُ

Rabbighfir warham innaka antal a'azzul akram

O Lord! Forgive and have mercy! Verily, You are the most Noble and most Honorable.

6. Dua when performing Rami (Pelting)

بِسْمِ اللهِ ، اللهُ أَكْبَرُ رَغْمًا لِلشَّيْطَانِ ، وَرِضًا لِلرَّحْمَانِ ، اَللّٰهُمَّ اجْعَلْهُ حَجًّا مَبْرُوْرًا ، وَذَنْبًا مَغْفُوْرًا ، وَسَعْيًا مَشْكُوْرًا

Bismillaahi Allaahu akbar raghman lish shaytaani wa ridhan lir rahmaani Allaahummaj'alhu hajjan mabrooran wa dhanban maghfooran wa sa'yan mashkooran

In the Name of Allah. Allah is the greatest. In defiance of the devil and to please the All Merciful. O Allah make this an accepted Hajj, and my sins to be forgiven, and my efforts to be rewarded.

7. Takbeer Tashreeq

اللهُ أَكْبَرُ اللهُ أَكْبَرُ ، لَا إِلٰهَ إِلَّا اللهُ وَاللهُ أَكْبَرُ ، اللهُ أَكْبَرُ وَلِلّٰهِ الْحَمْدُ

Allaahu Akbar, Allaahu Akbar, Laa Ilaaha Ilallaahu Wallaahu Akbar, Allaahu Akbar, Wa Lillaahil Hamd

Allah is the greatest, Allah is the greatest. There is none worthy of worship besides Allah and Allah is the greatest. Allah is the greatest and all praises are for Allah only.

AQEEDAH

Definition: Aqeedah is a set of beliefs that every muslim must believe in.

Status: It is necessary for a muslim to have faith in all these beliefs and it is also necessary for them to learn these beliefs.

❖ Allah

1. Allah is One.
2. He alone is worthy of worship. None besides Him is worthy of worship.
3. He has no partner.
4. Nothing is hidden from Him; He knows even the thoughts that go into a person's mind.
5. He knows everything that has happened and everything that will happen.
6. He is the Most Wise so whatever He does is out of ultimate wisdom.
7. He is the All Seeing and the All Hearing. He sees and hears everything.
8. He is the most powerful.
9. He created the earth, the skies, the sun, the moon, the stars, the angels, human beings, jinns and the whole universe.
10. He was not created by anyone.
11. He gives life and causes death.
12. He alone gives sustenance to all the creations and fulfills all their needs.
13. He does not eat, drink, tire, or sleep.
14. He is from eversince and will remain forever.
15. He does not have any parents, spouse, children, or any family.
16. He does not depend on anyone and everything depends on Him.
17. He resembles none. Nobody resembles Allah.
18. He is pure from all faults and defects.
19. He does not have hands, feet, nose, ears or a body like that of any creation.
20. We should therefore pray to Him for all our requirements.

The Beautiful Names of Allah ٱلْأَسْمَاءُ الْحُسْنَى

إِنَّ لِلَّهِ تَعَالَى تِسْعَةً وَتِسْعِيْنَ اسْمًا ، مَنْ أَحْصَاهَا دَخَلَ الْجَنَّةَ

The Messenger of Allah ﷺ said: *"Indeed, Allah has ninety nine names. Whoever memorizes them will enter paradise.* [Bukhaari]

هُوَ اللهُ الَّذِيْ لَا إِلَهَ إِلَّا هُوَ

اَلْمُتَكَبِّرُ · The Tremendous	اَلْجَبَّارُ The Most Powerful	اَلْعَزِيْزُ The Most Honorable	اَلْمُهَيْمِنُ The Protector	اَلْمُؤْمِنُ The Affirmer of Truth	اَلسَّلَامُ The Source of Peace	اَلْقُدُّوْسُ The Most Pure	اَلْمَلِكُ The True King	اَلرَّحِيْمُ · The Most Merciful	اَلرَّحْمٰنُ The Most Beneficent
اَلْقَابِضُ The Restrainer	اَلْعَلِيْمُ · The All Knowing	اَلْفَتَّاحُ The Victory Giver	اَلرَّزَّاقُ The Ever Providing	اَلْوَهَّابُ The Bestower	اَلْقَهَّارُ · The All Dominant	اَلْغَفَّارُ The Ever Forgiving	اَلْمُصَوِّرُ The Fashioner	اَلْبَارِئُ The Rightful	اَلْخَالِقُ The Creator
اَللَّطِيْفُ The Subtly Kind	اَلْعَدْلُ The Utterly Just	اَلْحَكَمُ The Judge	اَلْبَصِيْرُ · The All Seeing	اَلسَّمِيْعُ The All Hearing	اَلْمُذِلُّ The Giver of Dishonor	اَلْمُعِزُّ The Giver of Honor	اَلرَّافِعُ The Exalter	اَلْخَافِضُ The Abaser	اَلْبَاسِطُ The Expander
اَلْحَسِيْبُ The Reckoner	اَلْمُقِيْتُ The Sustainer	اَلْحَافِظُ The Preserver	اَلْكَبِيْرُ · The Most Great	اَلْعَلِيُّ The Most High	اَلشَّكُوْرُ The Rewarder	اَلْغَفُوْرُ The All Forgiving	اَلْعَظِيْمُ The Most Magnificent	اَلْحَلِيْمُ The Most Forbearant	اَلْخَبِيْرُ · The All Aware
اَلشَّهِيْدُ · The Witness	اَلْبَاعِثُ The Raiser of the Dead	اَلْمَجِيْدُ The Most Glorious	اَلْوَدُوْدُ The Most Loving	اَلْحَكِيْمُ · The Most Wise	اَلْوَاسِعُ The All Encompassing	اَلْمُجِيْبُ The Answerer	اَلرَّقِيْبُ The Watchful	اَلْكَرِيْمُ · The Generous	اَلْجَلِيْلُ The Most Majestic
اَلْمُحْيِي The Giver of Life	اَلْمُعِيْدُ The Restorer	اَلْمُبْدِئُ The Originator	اَلْمُحْصِي The Accounter	اَلْحَمِيْدُ The All Praiseworthy	اَلْوَلِيُّ The Protecting Friend	اَلْمَتِيْنُ · The Most Firm	اَلْقَوِيُّ The Most Strong	اَلْوَكِيْلُ The Dependable	اَلْحَقُّ The Truth
اَلْمُقْتَدِرُ The Dominant	اَلْقَادِرُ The All Able	اَلصَّمَدُ The Eternally Besought	اَلْأَحَدُ The One	اَلْوَاحِدُ The Unique	اَلْمَاجِدُ The Illustrious	اَلْوَاجِدُ The Perceiver	اَلْقَيُّوْمُ · The Self-Sufficient	اَلْحَيُّ The Ever Living	اَلْمُمِيْتُ The Giver of Death
اَلتَّوَّابُ The Acceptor of Repentance	اَلْبَرُّ The Most Kind	اَلْمُتَعَالِي The Sublime	اَلْوَالِي The Patron	اَلْبَاطِنُ · The Hidden	اَلظَّاهِرُ The Manifest	اَلْآخِرُ The Last	اَلْأَوَّلُ The First	اَلْمُؤَخِّرُ The Delayer	اَلْمُقَدِّمُ The Advancer
اَلْمَانِعُ The Depriver	اَلْمُغْنِيُّ The Enricher	اَلْغَنِيُّ The Independent	اَلْجَامِعُ The Unifier	اَلْمُقْسِطُ The Equitable	ذُو الْجَلَالِ وَالْإِكْرَامِ · The Lord of Majesty & Splendor	مَالِكُ الْمُلْكِ The Ruler of all Kingdoms	اَلرَّءُوْفُ · The Compassionate	اَلْعَفُوُّ The Pardoner	اَلْمُنْتَقِمُ The Avenger
	اَلصَّبُوْرُ · The Timeless	اَلرَّشِيْدُ The Director	اَلْوَارِثُ The Inheritor of All	اَلْبَاقِيْ The Ever Enduring	اَلْبَدِيْعُ The Incomparable	اَلْهَادِيْ The Guide	اَلنُّوْرُ The Light	اَلنَّافِعُ · The Benefactor	اَلضَّارُّ The Afflictor

❖ The Angels (Malaaikah)

1. Allah created them out of light.
2. They are invisible to us.
3. They do not commit sin and do only what Allah has commanded them.
4. We do not know their exact number.
5. There are few which we know about, among them, there are 4 who are most famous:
    a. Jibraeel AS He would bring the message from Allah to the Prophets. He was the helper of the Prophets. He is the leader of all the Angels.
    b. Mikaeel AS He is in charge of Food and Rain with the command of Allah.
    c. The Angel of Death (Malakul Maut) He takes people's life with the command of Allah.
    d. Israfeel AS He will blow the trumpet (Soor) on the day of Qiyamah by the command of Allah.

❖ The Books of Allah

1. Allah sent many books to the Prophets for mankind's guidance.
2. The small books are known as Saheefah, and the big ones are known as Kitaab. Among them there are 4 which are most famous:
    a. Tawrah (Old Testament) revealed to Musa AS.
    b. Zaboor (Psalms) revealed to Dawood AS.
    c. Injeel (Bible) revealed to Isa AS.
    d. Quran (the final book of Allah) revealed to Muhammad ﷺ.
3. All other books besides the Quran were revealed at once, while the [Quran] was revealed over a period of 23 years.
4. We must believe in all the books, but the other books are no l[onger in] their original forms.
5. The Quran is the final book and it is still free from any [changes]. Allah has promised to safeguard it.

❖ The Messengers of Allah

1. Allah sent many messengers to this world from time to time to guide mankind. These messengers were known as Rasool and Nabi.
2. We do not know the names nor exact number of all the messengers that came to this world.
3. Rasool is a messenger that received a new Divine Law and/or Book from Allah and there were approximately 313 of them.
4. Nabi is a messenger that confirmed the previous Divine Law and there were approximately 124,000 of them.
5. The first of them is Aadam AS and the last and final one is Muhammad ﷺ
6. They were all human beings who were specifically chosen by Allah.
7. They are innocent (Ma'soom), they did not commit any sin.
8. They are able to perform miracles with the help of Allah.
9. 'Isa AS is not the son of God, or part of God, nor was he crucified then resurrected but rather he is another messenger and he was saved by Allah and he will return to fight Dajjal.
10. There is no one that will come after Muhammad ﷺ as a new Rasool or Nabi and he has the highest position of them all.

Among them, 25 of them were mentioned in the Quran:

The 25 Messengers mentioned in the Quran are:

1. Aadam AS
2. Idrees AS
3. Nooh AS
4. Hood AS
5. Saalih AS
6. Lut AS
7. Ibraheem AS
8. Ismaa'eel AS
9. Ishaq AS
10. Shu'ayb AS
11. Ya'qub AS
12. Yusuf AS
13. Ayyoob AS
14. Dhul Kifl AS
15. Yunus AS
16. Musa AS
17. Ilyaas AS
18. Al-Yasa' AS
19. Dawood AS
20. Sulaymaan AS
21. Zakariyyaa AS
22. Yahya AS
23. 'Uzayr AS
24. 'Isa AS
25. Muhammad ﷺ

The Names of Rasulullah ﷺ — أَسْمَاءُ النَّبِيِّ ﷺ

إِنَّ اللهَ وَمَلَئِكَتَهُ يُصَلُّونَ عَلَى النَّبِيِّ ، يَأَيُّهَا الَّذِينَ ءَامَنُوا صَلُّوا عَلَيْهِ وَسَلِّمُوا تَسْلِيمًا

"Indeed Allah and His angels showers blessing on the Nabi. O You who believe, Ask for blessings on him and salute him with a worthy salutation." (33:56)

صَلَّى اللهُ عَلَيْهِ وَعَلَى آلِهِ وَأَصْحَابِهِ وَبَارَكَ وَسَلَّمَ تَسْلِيمًا كَثِيرًا كَثِيرًا

طه Taahaa	عَاقِب The Last In Succession	حَاشِر The 'Gatherer	مَاح The Effacer	وَحِيْد The Unique	أَحِيْد His Name in the Tawrah	مَحْمُوْد The Most Highly Praised	حَامِد The Praiser	أَحْمَد The Praised One	مُحَمَّد The Most Praised One
اَلْقَابِض The Restrainer	قَيِّم The Upright One	نَبِيُّ الرَّحْمَة The Prophet of Mercy	رَسُوْلُ الرَّحْمَة The Messenger of Mercy	نَبِيّ The Prophet	رَسُوْل The Messenger	سَيِّد The Leader	طَيِّب The Good	مُطَهَّر The Purifier	طَاهِر The Pure
صَفِيُّ الله The Chosen of Allah	حَبِيْبُ الله The Beloved of Allah	مُزَّمِّل The One Wrapped Up	مُدَّثِّر The Covered One	إِكْلِيْل The Crown	كَامِل The Perfect One	رَسُوْلُ الرَّاحَة The Messenger of Comfort	رَسُوْلُ الْمَلَاحِم The Messenger Who Fought Battles	مُقَفِّي The Best Example	مُقْتَفٍ The Selected One
نَبِيُّ التَّوْبَة The Prophet of Repentance	مَنْصُوْر The Victorious One	نَاصِر The Helper	مُذَكِّر The Reminder	مُنْجِي The Saviour	مُحْيِي The Reviver	خَاتَمُ الرُّسُل The Seal of All Messengers	خَاتَمُ الْأَنْبِيَاء The Seal of All Prophets	كَلِيْمُ الله The Intimate of Allah	نَجِيُّ الله The Confidant of Allah
مُنْذِر The Admonisher	نَذِيْر The Warner	مُبَشِّر The Giver of Glad Tidings	بَشِيْر The Glad Tiding	مَشْهُوْد The Attestor	شَهِيْد The Witnessed	شَاهِد The Witnesser	شَهِيْر The Famous One	مَعْلُوْم The Known One	حَرِيْصٌ عَلَيْكُم The Watchful Over You
مُجَاب The Responded To	مُجِيْب The Responsive	مَدْعُوّ The Called One	دَاعٍ The Caller	مُنِيْر The Illuminated One	مَهْدِيّ The Rightly Guided One	هُدًى The Guidance	مِصْبَاح The Lantern	سِرَاج The Lamp	نُوْر The Light
مَكِيْن The Steadfast	مُكَرَّم The Honored	كَرِيْم The Generous	مَأْمُوْن The Trusted One	أَمِيْن The Trustworthy	قَوِيّ The Powerful	حَقّ The Truth	وَلِيّ The Friend	عَفُوّ The Pardoner	حَفِيّ The Affectionate One
رَحْمَة The Mercy	ذُوْ فَضْلٍ The Possessor of Grace	ذُوْ عِزَّةٍ The Possessor of Might	ذُوْ مَكَانَةٍ The Possessor of Firmness	ذُوْ حُرْمَةٍ The Possessor of Honor	ذُوْ قُوَّةٍ The Possessor of Power	وَصُوْل The Connection	مُؤَمَّل The One Hoped For	مُبِيْن The Evident One	مَتِيْن The Steadfast One
مُصْطَفَى The Chosen One	اَلنَّجْمُ الثَّاقِب The Piercing Star	عُرْوَةٌ وُثْقَى The Trusty Handhold	غِيَاث The Rescuer	غَيْث The Rain (of Mercy)	غَوْث The Support	بُشْرَى The Good News	قَدَمُ صِدْقٍ The Firm Foothold	مُطِيْع The Obedient One	مُطَاع The One Obeyed
	مُنْتَقَى The Selected One	مُجْتَبَى The Singled Out One	صِرَاطٌ مُسْتَقِيم The Straight Path	صِرَاطُ الله The Path of Allah	سَيْفُ الله The Sword of Allah	حِزْبُ الله The Party of Allah	ذِكْرُ الله The Remembrance of Allah	هَدِيَّةُ الله The Gift of Allah	نِعْمَةُ الله The Favor of Allah

❖ The Sahaabah: Companions of Rasulullah ﷺ

1. People who either saw Nabi ﷺ or stayed in his company, embraced Islam and died as Muslims are known as Sahaabi.
2. Nabi ﷺ said: *"All the Sahaabah are just and pious and whoever amongst them you shall follow, you shall be guided."* Even though they can commit sins, Allah has forgiven them and is pleased with them.
3. A non-Sahaabi can never be equal in rank to any Sahaabi, even the lowest ranked Sahaabi.
4. It is compulsory to show respect to all Sahaabah and to refrain from speaking ill of them.
5. They can be divided into two groups: 1) Muhaajiroon, those Sahaabah that migrated from Makkah and 2) Ansaar, those Sahaabah that were locals of Madinah that helped Nabi ﷺ and the Muhaajiroon. The Ansaar are comprised of two tribes: 1) Aws and 2) Khazraj.

❖ Fate (Taqdeer)

Allah has the knowledge of everything of the past and the future. All good things happen by Allah's will alone and no misfortune can happen except by the will of Allah. Therefore we should not despair over any misfortune or boast over any favor. This teaches us that we should be thankful to Allah for his favors and have patience over any misfortune.

❖ The Last Day (Qiyaamat)

This world will one day come to an end. Besides Allah Ta'ala no one knows the exact day when Qiyaamat will occur. Only this much is known that on one Friday after the major signs, Israfeel (AS) will be ordered to blow the SOOR (Trumpet). The sound will cause every living person or creature to die. The earth will be shaken up, the mountains will become like flakes of cotton wool, the sun and the moon will crash, the stars will lose their shine, and the whole universe will be destroyed.

❖ The Life After Death

After the day of Qiyaamat when everything will be destroyed, Hadhrat ISRAFEEL (AS) will be ordered to blow the SOOR (Trumpet) for the second time. Once again every person that lived on this earth from the time of Hadhrat AADAM (AS) up to the final day will be brought back to life. They will all gather before Allah Ta'ala for judgment in the MAIDAN HASHR (Field of Resurrection). They will have to give an account of all their deeds. The good will be blessed and rewarded with JANNAT (Paradise). The evil ones will be punished in JAHANNAM (Hell). Allah Ta'ala will forgive whomever He wishes, besides the Kuffaar (Disbelievers) and Mushrikeen (Polytheists) who will be punished eternally.

BASIC ISLAMIC KNOWLEDGE

❖ The 12 Islamic Months

The Islamic Calendar is a lunar calendar ie. dependent on moon sighting. So if the new moon is sighted after 29 days, the new month will begin, otherwise the month will have a full 30 days, resulting in the year having 354 or 355 days.

1. Al-Muharram   2. Safar   3. Rabee 'Ul-Awwal   4. Rabee 'Uth-Thani
5. Jumaadal-Oolaa   6. Jumaadal-Aakhirah   7. Rajab   8. Sha'baan
9. Ramadhan   10. Shawwaal   11. Dhul-Qa'dah   12. Dhul-Hijjah

The 4 Sacred Months: Allah says in the Quran: "Surely, the number of months according to Allah is twelve (as written) in the Book of Allah on the day He created the heavens and the Earth, of which there are Four Sacred Months." (9:36)

1. Al-Muharram   **11. Dhul-Qa'dah**
7. Rajab   **12. Dhul-Hijjah**

Important Dates:
- 10th of Al-Muharram - Day of 'Aashura.
- 27th of Safar - Nabi ﷺ left Makkah Mukarramah for migration.
- 1st or 2nd of Rabee 'Ul-Awwal - Demise of Nabi ﷺ.
- 8th or 9th of Rabee 'Ul-Awwal - Birth of Nabi ﷺ.
- 27th of Rajab - Believed to be the journey of Israa and Mi'raj.
- 15th of Sha'baan - Lailatul Baraa-ah (Night of Freedom from Hell).
- 21st, 23rd, 25th, 27th, 29th of Ramadhan - Lailatul Qadr (Night of Power) Beginning of Revelation.
- 1st of Shawwaal - Eid-ul-Fitr (Sadaqatul Fitr).
- 9th of Dhul-Hijjah - Day of 'Arafah.
- 10th of Dhul-Hijjah - Eid-ul-Adha (Qurbani).
- 11th, 12th, and 13th of Dhul-Hijjah - Days of Tashreeq.
- 13th, 14th, and 15th of every month - Days of Beedh (The Radiant Days).

❖ Halal & Haram Food

Halal is that which is permissible and lawful in Islam and Zabiha are the rules of slaughtering an animal to make it Halal for consumption.

- Conditions of Zabiha: At least three of the four main veins of the throat must be cut, with mentioning the name of Allah, slaughtered by a Muslim or believing Ahl Kitaab.
- Meat that has been slaughtered by machines does not meet these conditions, making the food Haram.
- Kosher and UD or KD symbols do not mean the food is Halal.
- If the status of the food is unknown, then do not eat the food.
- Similarly, a normal Halal sign does not mean the food is Halal. Only eat food that is certified to be Halal by a proper certification board of scholars.
- Eating Haram means that a person's good deeds will not be accepted for 40 days.
- That body which has been nourished by Haram will not enter Jannah!

Ahlus Sunnah Wal Jamaa'ah (Sunni):

The true followers of Nabi ﷺ and the Sahaabah (RADH). In terms of Fiqh, we are followers of one of the four Madhabs and in terms of Aqeedah, we are followers of one of the two schools.

❖ The 4 Main Madhabs of Fiqh

There were many Imaams of Fiqh, they are known as Fuqahaa. Among them there are 4 Imaams who are most famous and they have their own Madhab. These are the only 4 Madhab which remain till now, and we **must** follow one of these Madhab. We should not rely on our understanding of the Quran and Sunnah, but rather we should rely on the understanding of these highly qualified Imaams and their countless, well trained students.

1. Imaam Abu Hanifah (RA) Nu'maan bin Thabit (Imaam A'zam, the Greatest Imaam) - Imaam of The Hanafi Madhab. 80 AH - 150 AH
2. Imaam Shafi'i (RA) Muhammad bin Idrees - Imaam of The Shafi'i Madhab. 150 AH – 204 AH
3. Imaam Maalik bin Anas (RA) - Imaam of The Maaliki Madhab. 93 AH - 179 AH.
4. Imaam Ahmad bin Hanbal (RA) - Imaam of The Hanbali Madhab. 164 AH - 241 AH.

❖ The 2 Main Madhabs of Aqeedah

We follow one of these Imaams in those matters of Aqeedah that were discussed afterwards and not clearly mentioned in the Quran. They, in turn, took their beliefs from their teachers who took from the Sahaabah. We should **never** try to interpret through our own understanding but rather learn from learned scholars.

1. Imaam Maatureedi (RA) Abu Mansoor Muhammad 238 AH - 333 AH
2. Imaam Ash'ari (RA) Ismaa'eel bin Abi Muhammad 260 AH - 324 AH

❖ The 6 Famous Books of Hadith

There are many books of hadith that contain many authentic hadith, but these six are the most well known and taught around the world.

1. Saheeh Bukhaari by Imaam Muhammad Bukhaari. 194 AH - 256 AH
2. Saheeh Muslim by Imaam Muslim bin Hajjaaj. 206 AH - 261 AH
3. Sunan Abu Dawud by Imaam Abu Dawud Sulaymaan. 202 AH - 275 AH
4. Sunan Tirmidhi by Imaam Abu 'Isa Muhammad Tirmidhi. 209 AH - 279 AH
5. Sunan Nasai by Imaam Ahmad Nasai. 214 AH - 313 AH
6. Sunan Ibn Majah by Imaam Muhammad bin Yazeed bin Majah. 209 AH - 273 AH

❖ The 3 Holy Cities

1. Makkah Mukarramah - Located in Saudi Arabia and the birthplace of Rasulullah ﷺ. Location of the Ka'bah, the Qiblah of all Muslims around the world, and one Salaah offered here is multiplied by 100,000.
2. Madinah Munawwarah - Located in Saudi Arabia and the resting place of Rasulullah ﷺ. Location of Masjid Nabawi and one Salaah offered here is multiplied by 1,000.
3. Jerusalem - Located in Palestine and the resting place of many Messengers. Location of Masjid Aqsa, the original Qiblah, and one Salaah offered here is multiplied by 500.

❖ The Mahram

The Mahram are those women a man is allowed to see but is not allowed to marry. And for a woman, mahram are those men she can show her face to but she is not allowed to marry them. (Anyone besides these people; the laws of Hijab will apply on them.)

1. Parents, grandparents, and parent-in-laws
2. Children, grandchildren, and children-in-laws
3. Full and half siblings and their children (nephews and nieces)
4. Paternal and maternal uncles and aunts (but not their children ie. cousins)

100 SUNNAH & ETIQUETTES

☐ Sunnah of Drinking

1. Recite *Bismillaah* before drinking. (Tirmidhi)

2. Drink with the right hand. Do not drink with the left hand. (Muslim)

3. Sit and drink. Do not stand and drink. (Muslim)

4. Pour the drink into a glass first and then drink. Do not drink directly from the jug/container. (Tirmidhi)

5. Drink in 3 breaths/sips by removing the utensil from the mouth after each sip before taking another sip. Do not drink in one gulp. (Muslim)

6. One should not breathe/blow into the cup, rather breathe after moving it away from the mouth. (Bukhaari)

7. Recite the Dua after drinking water:

اَلْحَمْدُ لِلّٰهِ الَّذِيْ سَقَانَا عَذْبًا فُرَاتًا بِرَحْمَتِهِ ، وَلَمْ يَجْعَلْهُ مِلْحًا أُجَاجًا بِذُنُوْبِنَا

Alhamdulillaa hilladhee saqaanaa adhban furaatan birahmatihi walam yaj'alhu milhan ujaajan bidhunoobinaa

All praises are due to Allah, who gave us sweet and pleasant water to drink due to His mercy, and He did not make it salty and bitter due to our sins.

(Tabraani)

8. Recite the Dua after drinking milk: (Tirmidhi)

اَللّٰهُمَّ بَارِكْ لَنَا فِيْهِ ، وَزِدْنَا مِنْهُ

Allaahumma baarik lanaa feehe wa zidnaa minhu

O Allah! Grant us blessings in this and increase it for us.

9. To gargle the mouth after drinking milk. (Bukhaari, Ibn Majah)

10. Do not drink from gold or silver utensils. (Bukhaari)

☐ Sunnah of Eating

11. Eat while sitting on the floor in Tashahhud position. (Ibn Majah)

12. Spread out a cloth (Dastarkhaan) on the floor before eating. (Bukhaari)

13. Remove your shoes before eating. (Mustadrak Haakim)

14. Wash both hands before eating. (Abu Dawud)

15. Recite the Dua before eating: (Mustadrak Haakim)

بِسْمِ اللهِ ، وَبَرَكَةِ اللهِ

Bismillaahi wa barakatillaah

In the name of Allah and with the blessings of Allah.

16. If this Dua is not read at the beginning, then read this Dua when you remember: (Tirmidhi)

بِسْمِ اللهِ أَوَّلَهُ وَآخِرَهُ

Bismillaahi awwalahu wa aakhirahu

With Allah's name in the beginning and at the end.

17. When eating, sit with one knee raised or both knees raised. (Ibn Majah)

18. Do not lean and eat. (Bukhaari)

19. Eat with the right hand. (Bukhaari)

20. Eat with three fingers if possible. (Muslim)

21. To eat together as a group at one time. (Abu Dawud)

22. Eat from the side that is closest to you. Do not start from the center. (Muslim)

23. Do not find fault with the food. Leave that which you do not like. (Muslim)

24. Do not blow on the food. (Musnad Ahmad)

25. To pick up any food that has fallen and to eat it after cleaning it. (Muslim)

26. After eating, lick the fingers three times. (Muslim)

27. Clean/lick the plate and other utensils thoroughly after eating. (Muslim)

28. Wash both hands after eating. (Bukhaari)

29. Rinse the mouth after eating. (Bukhaari)

30. Recite the Duaas after eating:

اَلْحَمْدُ لِلَّهِ الَّذِيْ أَطْعَمَنَا وَسَقَانَا وَجَعَلَنَا مُسْلِمِيْنَ

Alhamdulillaa hilladhee at'amanaa wa saqaanaa wa ja'alanaa muslimeen.

All praises are due to Allah, who gave us food and drink and made us Muslims. (Abu Dawud)

اَلْحَمْدُ لِلَّهِ حَمْدًا كَثِيْرًا ، طَيِّبًا مُبَارَكًا فِيْهِ ، غَيْرَ مَكْفِيٍّ ، وَلَا مُوَدَّعٍ ، وَلَا مُسْتَغْنًى عَنْهُ ، رَبَّنَا

Alhamdulillaahi hamdan katheeran twayyiban mubaarakan feeh ghaira makfeeyin walaa muwadda'in walaa mustaghnan 'anhu rabbanaa

All praises are due to Allah, such praises which are abundant and full of blessings. We are not lifting this food regarding it to be sufficient, or bidding it farewell, or expressing no need for it. O our Sustainer! (Bukhaari)

اَلْحَمْدُ لِلَّهِ الَّذِيْ أَطْعَمَنِيْ هَذَا ، وَرَزَقَنِيْهِ مِنْ غَيْرِ حَوْلٍ مِنِّيْ وَلَا قُوَّةٍ

Alhamdulillaa hilladhee at'amanee haadhaa warazaqaneehi min ghair hawlim minnee quwwah

All praises are due to Allah who has fed me this food and has granted it to me without any strength or ability of my own. (Tirmidhi)

☐ Sunnah of Sleeping

31. To sleep in the state of Wudhu. (Bukhaari)
32. To brush the teeth with a Miswaak. (Bukhaari)
33. To recite *Bismillaah* whilst closing the doors or locking them. (Bukhaari)
34. To sleep early at night (after 'Ishaa). (Bukhaari)
35. To dust the bedding 3 times before sleeping. (Bukhaari)
36. Make Tawbah (ask Allah to forgive your sins) before sleeping. (Tirmidhi)
37. To remove jealousy and enmity from one's heart. (Tirmidhi)

38. Recite the Duaas before sleeping:

اَللّٰهُمَّ بِاسْمِكَ أَمُوْتُ وَأَحْيَى

Allaahumma bismika amooto wa ahyaa.

O Allah! With Your name I die and I live. (Bukhaari)

اَلْحَمْدُ لِلّٰهِ الَّذِيْ أَطْعَمَنَا وَسَقَانَا ، وَكَفَانَا ، وَآوَانَا ، فَكَمْ مِمَّنْ لَا كَافِيَ لَهُ وَلَا مُؤْوِيَ

Alhamdulillaa hilladhee at'amanaa wa saqaanaa wa kafaanaa wa aawaanaa fakam mimman laa kaafiya lahu wa laa mu-wiya

All praises are due to Allah, who gave us food and drink and who sufficed us and who sheltered us; for how many have none to suffice them or shelter them. (Muslim)

بِسْمِ اللهِ وَضَعْتُ جَنْبِيْ ، اَللّٰهُمَّ اغْفِرْ لِيْ ذَنْبِيْ ، وَأَخْسِئْ شَيْطَانِيْ ، وَفُكَّ رِهَانِيْ ، وَاجْعَلْنِيْ فِي النَّدِيِّ الْأَعْلَى

Bismillaahi wadhwa'tu janbee allaahummaghfirlee dhanbee wa-akhsi- shaytwaanee wafukka rihaanee waj'alnee fin nadiyyil a'alaa

In the name of Allah, I lie down. O Allah, forgive my sins, ward off from me my shaytan, free me from my obligations (to others), and enter me into the loftiest assembly (of angels). (Abu Dawud)

39. To recite Aayatul Kursi. (Bukhaari)

40. To recite Surah Kafiroon. (Abu Dawud)

41. To recite Surah Ikhlas, Surah Falaq, and Surah Naas 3 times and then blow over the body. (Bukhaari)

42. To recite the Tasbih Fatimi. (Abu Dawud)

43. To recite Surah Mulk and Surah Sajdah. (Tirmidhi)

44. To recite Surah Zumar and Surah Bani Israeel. (Tirmidhi)

45. To recite the last two verses of Surah Baqarah. (Bukhaari)

46. To sleep on the right side facing the Qiblah if possible. (Abu Dawud)

47. To sleep with the right hand under the cheek. (Bukhaari)

48. Do not sleep on the stomach. (Abu Dawud)

49. Do not sleep on the back when there is fear of exposing the Satr. (Tirmidhi)

50. Wake up early to pray 8 Rakaats of Tahajjud before Fajr. (Bukhaari)

☐ Sunnah of Awakening

51. Rub both palms on the face & eyes so that the sleep disappears. (Bukhaari)

52. Recite the last ten verses of Surah Aal 'Imran. (Muslim)

53. Recite the Duaas upon awakening:

اَلْحَمْدُ لِلّٰهِ الَّذِيْ أَحْيَانَا بَعْدَ مَا أَمَاتَنَا ، وَإِلَيْهِ النُّشُوْرُ

Alhamdulillaah hilladhee ahyaanaa ba'da maa amaatanaa wa ilayhin nushoor.

All praises are due to Allah, who gave us life after taking it from us, and to Him is the resurrection. (Bukhaari)

اَلْحَمْدُ لِلّٰهِ الَّذِيْ عَافَانِيْ فِيْ جَسَدِيْ ، وَرَدَّ عَلَيَّ رُوْحِيْ ، وَأَذِنَ لِيْ بِذِكْرِهِ

Alhamdulillaah hilladhee 'aafaanee fee jasadee waradda 'alayya roohee wa-adhina lee bidhikrih

All praises are due to Allah, who granted me wellbeing in my body, and returned my soul to me, and allowed me to remember Him. (Tirmidhi)

54. To brush the teeth with a Miswaak. (Musnad Ahmad, Abu Dawud)

55. Wash both hands till the wrist 3 times before dipping it into a vessel. (Muslim)

56. Rinse the nose with water 3 times. (Bukhaari)

57. To perform Wudhu. (Bukhaari)

58. To pray two Rakaats. (Bukhaari)

59. Recite Surah Yaseen for the fulfillment of the needs of the day. (Daarimi)

60. Start the day off with the recitation of the Quran. (Abu Dawud)

☐ Sunnah of Leaving & Entering the Home

61. To say Salaam to the members of the household when you are leaving the house. (Bukhaari)

62. Recite the Duaas of leaving the home:

بِسْمِ اللهِ تَوَكَّلْتُ عَلَى اللهِ ، وَلَا حَوْلَ وَلَا قُوَّةَ إِلَّا بِاللهِ

Bismillaahi tawakkaltu 'alallaah wa laa hawla wa laa quwwata illaa billaah.

In the name of Allah, I have placed my trust in Allah. There is no power and might except from Allah. (Abu Dawud)

اَللّٰهُمَّ إِنِّيْ أَعُوْذُبِكَ أَنْ أَضِلَّ أَوْ أُضَلَّ ، أَوْ أَزِلَّ أَوْ أُزَلَّ ، أَوْ أَظْلِمَ أَوْ أُظْلَمَ ، أَوْ أَجْهَلَ أَوْ يُجْهَلَ عَلَيَّ

Allaahumma innee a'oodhubika an adhwilla aw udhwalla aw azilla aw uzalla aw azhlima aw uzhlama aw ajhala aw ujhala 'alayy

O Allah, I seek Your protection from misguiding others or being misguided, from erring or others causing me to err, from oppressing others or being oppressed, and from acting ignorantly or others acting ignorantly to me.

(Tirmidhi)

63. Look towards the sky when reciting the Duaas. (Abu Dawud)

64. To leave the house with the left foot. (Bukhaari)

65. To enter the house with the right foot. (Bukhaari)

66. To read any Dhikr of Allah whilst entering the house. (Muslim)

67. Recite the Duaas of entering the home: (Abu Dawud)

اَللّٰهُمَّ إِنِّيْ أَسْئَلُكَ خَيْرَ الْمَوْلَجِ وَخَيْرَ الْمَخْرَجِ ، بِسْمِ اللهِ وَلَجْنَا ، وَبِسْمِ اللهِ خَرَجْنَا ، وَعَلَى اللهِ رَبِّنَا تَوَكَّلْنَا

Allaahumma innee as-aluka khairal mawlaji wa khairal makhraji Bismillaahi walajnaa wa Bismillaahi kharajnaa wa'alallaahi rabbinaa tawakkalnaa.

O Allah, I ask You for the best entrance and the best exit. In the name of Allah we enter, and in the name of Allah we leave, and in Allah our Lord do we trust.

68. To announce one has arrived at home by knocking or coughing, etc. (Nasai)

69. Salaam should be said upon entering the house. (Tirmidhi)

70. To use a Miswaak after entering the house. (Muslim, Abu Dawud)

☐ Sunnah of Clothing

71. Wear white clothes. (Abu Dawud, Tirmidhi)

72. Do not wear clothes to show off to attract people's attention. (Abu Dawud)

73. Do not wear clothes that have pictures of animate objects. (Bukhaari)

74. Begin wearing clothes/shoes from the right side. (Tirmidhi)

75. Begin removing clothes/shoes from the left side. (Tirmidhi)

76. Lift the shoes with the thumb and index finger of the left hand. (Tabraani)

77. Men should wear a Qamees, a long, loose fitting shirt with buttons, sleeves, a collar, and which reaches below the knees and above the ankles. (Abu Dawud)

78. Men should wear a white hat/topee. (Tabraani)

79. Men should wear a turban. (Muslim)

80. Men are not allowed to have the clothes go below their ankles. (Bukhaari)

81. Men are not allowed to wear silk or gold jewelry. (Bukhaari)

82. Females should cover their ankles with their clothes. (Tirmidhi)

83. Females should cover their entire body, face, and hair. (Bukhaari)

84. Men should not resemble women (including jewelry and accessories) and women should not resemble men. (Bukhaari)

85. Recite the Dua of changing clothes and Duaas of wearing new clothes:

اَلْحَمْدُ لِلّٰهِ الَّذِيْ كَسَانِيْ هٰذَا الثَّوْبَ ، وَرَزَقَنِيْهِ مِنْ غَيْرِ حَوْلٍ مِنِّيْ وَلَا قُوَّةٍ

Alhamdulillaa hilladhee kasaanee haadhaath thawba warazaqaneehi min ghair hawlim minnee quwwah

All praises are due to Allah who has clothed me with this garment and has granted it to me without any strength or ability of my own. (Abu Dawud)

اَللّٰهُمَّ لَكَ الْحَمْدُ أَنْتَ كَسَوْتَنِيْهِ ، أَسْأَلُكَ مِنْ خَيْرِهِ وَخَيْرِ مَا صُنِعَ لَهُ ، وَأَعُوْذُ بِكَ مِنْ شَرِّهِ وَشَرِّ مَا صُنِعَ لَهُ

Allaahumma lakal hamdu anta kasawtaneehi as-aluka min khairihi wa khair maa swuni'a lahu wa a'oodhubika min sharrihi wa sharri naa swuni'a lahu

O Allah, for You is all praise. You have clothed me with this. I ask You for its good and the good of that for which it was made and I seek Your protection from its evil and the evil of that for which it was made. (Tirmidhi)

اَلْحَمْدُ لِلَّهِ الَّذِيْ كَسَانِيْ مَا أُوَارِيْ بِهِ عَوْرَتِيْ وَأَتَجَمَّلُ بِهِ فِيْ حَيَاتِيْ

Alhamdulillaa hilladhee kasaanee maa uwaaree bihi 'awratee wa atajammalu bihi fee hayaatee

All praises are due to Allah who has clothed me with something to cover my nakedness and beautify myself in my lifetime. (Tirmidhi)

☐ Miscellaneous Sunnah

86. To keep the gaze on the ground whilst walking.

87. To speak softly and politely.

88. To greet all Muslims with, "*Assalaamu 'alaikum wa rahmatullaahi wa barakaatuh*" and to meet them with a cheerful face.

89. To show mercy to those who are younger than you and to respect your elders and your parents.

90. To visit a Muslim when he is sick.

91. To be good towards your neighbor.

92. To care for the poor and needy.

93. To keep good relations with all your relatives.

94. To honor a guest, even though he may not be of a very high position.

95. To exchange gifts with one another.

96. To make Mashwarah (consult) with one's parents, teachers, or elders before doing any work.

97. To ponder over the creation of Allah Ta'ala.

98. To command people to do good and to forbid them from doing evil.

99. To recite some portion of the Quran daily.

100. To make Dua to Allah for the fulfillment of one's needs in any language.

HOW SHOULD I SPEND MY DAY?

1. Wake up in the morning, reciting the Duaas after awakening.
2. Brush your teeth thoroughly.
3. Make Wudhu and perform your Fajr Salaah (in the Masjid).
4. Make Dua for a few minutes in your own language.
5. Ask Allah Ta'ala to make the day's work easy for you.
6. Recite the morning Duaas.
7. Recite Durood Shareef and Istighfar 100 times each.
8. Recite Surah Yaseen.
9. Get ready for school.
10. Put on your clothes following the Sunnahs of clothing.
11. Have a good breakfast so that you will be fresh for the day.
12. Check that you have all your books and stationery.
13. Make Salaam and kiss your parents when leaving home.
14. At school, respect and listen to your teacher.
15. Be friendly with your classmates.
16. Do not fight and argue with anyone.
17. After school, go straight home.
18. Make Salaam when you enter.
19. Perform your Dhuhr Salaah (in the Masjid).
20. Have something to eat and go early to Madrasah.
21. Correct your intention. Our intention must be that we came to learn about Allah Ta'ala and Nabi ﷺ and practice upon what we had learnt.
22. Read the Duaas before entering and before leaving the home and masjid.
23. Respect the teacher and complete all your lessons.
24. Perform your 'Asr Salaah at Madrasah.
25. After Madrasah, go straight home.

26. Make Salaam when you enter and give your parents a big hug.
27. Rest a while and speak nicely to your brothers and sisters.
28. Ask your parents if they need any help around the house.
29. Perform your Maghrib Salaah (in the Masjid).
30. Make special Dua for yourself, your family, and all the Muslims.
31. Recite the evening Duaas.
32. Recite Surah Waqi'ah.
33. Lay out the Dastarkhaan (eating cloth) and prepare for dinner.
34. Eat together with your family while following the Sunnahs of eating.
35. Have a few minutes of Ta'leem (Hadith reading) before or after dinner.
36. Help your parents clean up, wash the plates, and throw out the garbage.
37. Then get down to doing your homework.
38. First revise your Madrasah Sabaq (lesson).
39. Then complete all your homework for school and Madrasah.
40. Help your siblings with their homework and do not fight with them.
41. Perform your 'Ishaa Salaah (in the Masjid).
42. Sit with your parents and family.
43. Tell them what you learnt for the day and ask about their day.
44. Ask your parents to make special Dua for you.
45. Make sure you have everything ready for tomorrow.
46. Get ready to sleep while following the Sunnahs of sleeping.
47. Think about what you did today and what you can improve on.
48. Read the Duaas before sleeping.
49. Have a good night's sleep.
50. Try to wake up early for Tahajjud.

HADITH

Definition: Hadith are the sayings, actions, and approvals of our beloved Rasulullah ﷺ.

Status: It is necessary to live our lives according to the Sunnah of Rasulullah ﷺ and to do as he commanded and to stay away from what he prohibited.

"So take what the Messenger assigns to you, and refrain from what he has forbidden you from." (59:07)

Level 1

Correct Intentions
Innamal Aa'maalu binniyyaat   إِنَّمَا الْأَعْمَالُ بِالنَّيَّاتِ

1. Actions are dependent on their intentions.

Sincerity
Addeenun Nasweehah   اَلدِّيْنُ النَّصِيْحَةُ

2. Islam is to act with sincerity.

Good Character
Albirru Husnul Khuluq   اَلْبِرُّ حُسْنُ الْخُلُقِ

3. Righteousness is good character.

Cleanliness
Attwuhooru shatrul Eemaan   اَلطُّهُوْرُ شَطْرُ الْإِيْمَانِ

4. Purity is half of faith.

Good Speech
Alkalimatut Twayyibatu Swadaqatun   اَلْكَلِمَةُ الطَّيِّبَةُ صَدَقَةٌ

5. It is a charity to say a good word.

Level 2
Love

Almar-u ma'a man Ahabba   اَلْمَرْءُ مَعَ مَنْ أَحَبَّ

6. A person will be with whom he loves.

Controlling Anger

Laa Taghdhwab   لَا تَغْضَبْ

7. Do not become angry.

Harm of Deception

Man Ghassha falaysa minnaa   مَنْ غَشَّ فَلَيْسَ مِنَّا

8. Whoever deceives us is not one of us.

Compassion

Almu'minu mir-aatul mu'min   اَلْمُؤْمِنُ مِرْآةُ الْمُؤْمِنِ

9. A believer is a mirror of another believer.

Importance of Wudhu

Miftaahus Salaatil Wudhu   مِفْتَاحُ الصَّلَاةِ الْوُضُوءُ

10. Wudhu is the key to Salaah.

Importance of Fasting

Asswiyaamu junnatun   اَلصِّيَامُ جُنَّةٌ

11. Fasting is a shield.

Steadfastness

Qul Aamantu billahi thummas taqim   قُلْ: آمَنْتُ بِاللهِ ثُمَّ اسْتَقِمْ

12. Say: "I believe in Allah," then remain steadfast.

Importance of Dua

Addu'aa-o huwal 'ibaadah   اَلدُّعَاءُ هُوَ الْعِبَادَةِ

13. Duaa itself is a form of worship.

Fear of Allah

Ittaqillaaha Haythumaa Kunta   اِتَّقِ اللهَ حَيْثُمَا كُنْتَ

14. Have fear and be conscious of Allah wherever you may be.

Virtue of Good Deeds

Atbi'is sayyi-atal hasanata tamhuhaa   أَتْبِعِ السَّيِّئَةَ الْحَسَنَةَ تَمْحُهَا

15. Follow up a bad deed with a good deed, it will wipe it out.

Good Conduct

Khaliqin Naasa bi khuluqin hasan   خَالِقِ النَّاسَ بِخُلُقٍ حَسَنٍ

16. Treat people with good conduct.

Virtue of the Quran

Al Qur-aanu hujjatun laka aw 'alayka   اَلْقُرْآنُ حُجَّةٌ لَكَ أَوْ عَلَيْكَ

17. The Quran will be evidence for you or against you.

Harm of Oppression

Azh zhulmu zhulumaatun yawmal qiyaamah   اَلظُّلْمُ ظُلُمَاتٌ يَوْمَ الْقِيَامَةِ

18. Injustice will be a darkness on the Day of Judgement.

Virtue of Repentance

Attaa-ibu minadh dhanbi kaman laa dhanba lahu   اَلتَّائِبُ مِنَ الذَّنْبِ كَمَنْ لَا ذَنْبَ لَهُ

19. The one who repents from sins is like the one who is sinless.

Consideration of Others

Tumeetul adhaa 'anit twareeqi swadaqatun   تُمِيطُ الأَذَى عَنِ الطَّرِيْقِ صَدَقَةٌ

20. Removing a harmful object from the path is a charity.

Level 3

Abstinence From Worldly Pleasures

Addunyaa sijnul mu-mini wa jannatul kafir   اَلدُّنْيَا سِجْنُ الْمُؤْمِنِ وَجَنَّةُ الْكَافِرِ

21. This world is a prison for the believer and a paradise for the nonbelievers.

Harm of Imitation

Man Tashabbaha biqawmin fahuwa minhum   مَنْ تَشَبَّهَ بِقَوْمٍ فَهُوَ مِنْهُمْ

22. Whoever imitates a (group of) people will be one of them.

Virtue of Knowledge

Man yuridillaahu bikhayrin yufaqqih hu fiddeen   مَنْ يُرِدِ اللهُ بِخَيْرٍ يُفَقِّهْهُ فِي الدِّيْنِ

23. Whoever Allah wants goodness for, he grants him the understanding of Deen.

Virtue of Charity

Alyadul 'Ulyaa khayrun minal yadis suflaa   اَلْيَدُ الْعُلْيَا خَيْرٌ مِنَ الْيَدِ السُّفْلَى

24. The upper (giving) hand is better than the lower (receiving) hand.

Virtue of Patience

Innamas swabru 'indas swadamatil oolaa   إِنَّمَا الصَّبْرُ عِنْدَ الصَّدَمَةِ الْأُوْلَى

25. The real patience is at the first stroke of calamity.

Giving Glad Tidings

يَسِّرُوا وَلَا تُعَسِّرُوا وَبَشِّرُوا وَلَا تُنَفِّرُوا

Yassiroo walaa tu'assiroo wabashiroo walaa tunaffiroo

26. Make matters easy (for the people) and do not make it difficult and give glad tidings and do not repulse them.

Abstinence from Frivolity

مِنْ حُسْنِ إِسْلَامِ الْمَرْءِ تَرْكُهُ مَا لَا يَعْنِيْهِ

Min husni Islaamil mar-i tarkuhu maa laa ya'neehi

27. It is from the excellence of one's Islam that he leaves that which is of no concern to him.

Virtue of Consistency

أَحَبُّ الْأَعْمَالِ إِلَى اللهِ أَدْوَمُهَا وَإِنْ قَلَّ

Ahabbul a'maali ilallaahi adwamuhaa wa in qalla

28. The most beloved of deeds to Allah are those done with consistency, even if they are small.

Importance of the Neighbor

لَا يَدْخُلُ الْجَنَّةَ مَنْ لَا يَأْمَنُ جَارُهُ بَوَائِقَهُ

Laa yadkhulul jannata man laa ya-manu jaaruhu bawaa-iqah

29. That person will not enter Paradise whose neighbor is not secure from his mischief.

Virtue of Concealing

مَنْ سَتَرَ مُسْلِمًا سَتَرَهُ اللهُ فِي الدُّنْيَا وَالْآخِرَةِ

Man satara musliman satarahullaaahu fiddunyaa wal aakhirah

30. Whoever covers the faults of a Muslim, Allah will cover his faults in this world and the hereafter.

Virtue of Mercy

إِرْحَمُوا مَنْ فِي الْأَرْضِ يَرْحَمْكُمْ مَنْ فِي السَّمَاءِ

Irhamoo man fil ardhi yarhamkum man fis samaa

31. Be merciful to those on the Earth and the one in the Heaven will be merciful to you.

Virtue of Aid

اللهُ فِيْ عَوْنِ الْعَبْدِ مَا كَانَ الْعَبْدُ فِيْ عَوْنِ أَخِيْهِ

Allaahu fii 'awnil 'abdi maa kaanal 'abdu fii 'awni akheeh

32. Allah will be in the aid of his servant so long as he is in the aid of his brother.

Virtue of Mutual Love

لَا يُؤْمِنُ أَحَدُكُمْ حَتَّى يُحِبَّ لِأَخِيْهِ مَا يُحِبُّ لِنَفْسِهِ

Laa yu-minu ahadukum hattaa yuhibbu li-akheehi maa yuhibbu linafsih

33. None of you are true believers until he loves for his brother what he loves for himself.

Harm of Pride

لَا يَدْخُلُ الْجَنَّةَ مَنْ كَانَ فِيْ قَلْبِهِ مِثْقَالُ ذَرَّةٍ مِنْ كِبْرٍ

Laa yadkhulul jannata man kaana fii qalbihi mithqaalu dharratin min kibrin

34. Anyone who has an atom's weight of arrogance in his heart will not enter paradise.

Good Speech

مَنْ كَانَ يُؤْمِنُ بِاللهِ وَالْيَوْمِ الْآخِرِ فَلْيَقُلْ خَيْرًا أَوْ لِيَصْمُتْ

Man kaana yu-minu billaahi wal yawmil aakhiri falyaqul khayran aw liyasmut

35. The person who believes in Allah and the Last Day should either speak good or stay silent.

Importance of Salaah

سُئِلَ النَّبِيُّ: أَيُّ الْأَعْمَالِ أَحَبُّ إِلَى اللهِ؟ قَالَ: اَلصَّلَاةُ عَلى وَقْتِهَا

Su-ilan Nabiyyu Ayyul a'maali ahabbu ilallaah qaala as swalaatu 'alaa waqtihaa

36. Rasulullah was asked: "Which act is the dearest to Allah?" He replied: "Salaah at its appointed time."

Controlling Anger

لَيْسَ اَلشَّدِيْدُ بِالصُّرَعَةِ إِنَّمَا اَلشَّدِيْدُ الَّذِيْ يَمْلِكُ نَفْسَهُ عِنْدَ الْغَضَبِ

Laysash shadeedu bis swur'ati innamash shadeeduladhee yamliku nafsahu 'indal ghadhab

37. The strong person is not the one who overcomes the people by his strength, rather the strong person is the one who controls himself at the time of anger.

Importance of Actions

إِنَّ اللهَ لَا يَنْظُرُ إِلَى صُوَرِكُمْ وَأَمْوَالِكُمْ وَلَكِنْ يَنْظُرُ إِلَى قُلُوبِكُمْ وَأَعْمَالِكُمْ

Innallaaha laa yanzhuru ilaa swuwarikum wa amwaalikum wa laakin yanzhuru ilaa quloobikum wa a'amaalikum

38. Allah does not look at your appearance or wealth rather he looks at your hearts and actions.

Virtue of Truthfulness and Harm of Lying

إِنَّ الصِّدْقَ يَهْدِيْ إِلَى الْبِرِّ وَإِنَّ الْبِرَّ يَهْدِيْ إِلَى الْجَنَّةِ وَإِنَّ الْكَذِبَ يَهْدِيْ إِلَى الْفُجُورِ وَإِنَّ الْفُجُورَ يَهْدِيْ إِلَى النَّارِ

Innas swidqa yahdee ilal bir wa innal birra yahdee ilal jannah wa innal kadhiba yahdee ilal fujoor wa innal fujoor yahdee ilan naar

39. Truthfulness leads to righteousness and righteousness leads to paradise. Lying leads to deviance and deviance leads to Hell.

Virtue of Dhikr

كَلِمَتَانِ خَفِيفَتَانِ عَلَى اللِّسَانِ ثَقِيلَتَانِ فِي الْمِيزَانِ حَبِيبَتَانِ إِلَى الرَّحْمَنِ: سُبْحَانَ اللهِ وَبِحَمْدِهِ سُبْحَانَ اللهِ الْعَظِيمِ

Kalimataani khafeefataani 'alal lisaan thaqeelataani fil meezaan habeebataani ilar rahmaan subhaanallaahi wabihamdihi subhaanallaahil azheem

40. Two phrases are loved by Allah, and are light on the tongue while heavy on the scale (of good deeds): " (Glory is to Allah, and praise is to him, Allah the greatest is free from imperfection).

The Messenger of Allah ﷺ said:
"May Allah bless a man who hears a hadith from us and memorizes it so that he can convey it to others, for perhaps he is conveying it to one who will understand it better than him, and perhaps the one who conveys knowledge does not understand it himself."
[Tirmidhi, Abu Dawud]

SEERAH

Definition: Seerah is the biography and life story of our beloved Rasulullah ﷺ.

Status: It is necessary to learn about the life of Rasulullah ﷺ and to lead our life according to how he led his life.

"There is indeed a good model for you in the Messenger of Allah - for the one who has hope in Allah and the Last Day, and remembers Allah profusely." (33:21)

BRIEF SEERAH OF THE PROPHET MUHAMMAD ﷺ

Lesson 1

The Prophet Muhammad ﷺ was born in Makkah Mukarramah on Rabee 'Ul-Awwal, April 571 A.D.; this was the same year in which Abraha, Governor of Yemen, tried to destroy the Ka'bah. The demise of Abdullah, the father of the Prophet ﷺ, took place before the birth of the Prophet ﷺ. The Prophet's mother, Aaminah, sent him to Haleemah (RADH), from the tribe of Sa'd, so that he may be weaned and brought up by her. The first splitting of the Prophet's heart also took place during this time.

Lesson 2

The Prophet ﷺ spent four years in the tribe of Sa'd, after which he went to his grandparent's house with his respected mother. The Prophet's mother passed away on the way to Makkah Mukarramah in a place called 'Abwa'. The Prophet ﷺ was 6 years old at that time. Umme Ayman, the female servant of the Prophet's mother, brought him back to Makkah Mukarramah. 'Abdul Muttalib, the grandfather of the Prophet ﷺ, took him into his care. The Prophet ﷺ was 8 years old when his grandfather passed away. His uncle Abu Talib was then blessed with the opportunity to look after him. He took the Prophet ﷺ to Syria when he was 12 years old. Three years later when the Prophet's age was 15, the incident of Hilful Fudhool (Alliance of the Virtuous) took place.

Lesson 3

The second time the Prophet ﷺ traveled to Syria was for business when he was 25 years old. He had gone at the request of Khadijah (RADH). The Prophet ﷺ married Khadijah (RADH) after he returned from Syria. The Prophet held a high status amongst the Quraysh and was therefore respected very much by them. They even chose him to be the judge regarding the black stone when a war almost broke out due to everyone wanting the honor of placing the black stone within the Ka'bah wall. The Prophet was 35 years old when this event took place.

Lesson 4

When the Prophet ﷺ was 40 years old, the first Wahy (revelation) was revealed to him at the cave of Hira in Jabal Noor and he was blessed with the gift of prophethood. When the Prophet started to preach openly in accordance to Allah's order, the disbelievers started to torture and intimidate those who responded to his call, therefore some of companions were forced to migrate to Habashah (Absyinnia).

Lesson 5

The Prophet ﷺ was 50 years old when Abu Talib passed away and not long after, Khadijah (RADH) also passed away. The disbelievers now started to trouble the Prophet ﷺ so much that he made intention to travel to Taif. When the Prophet ﷺ preached in Taif, he came across the same kind of hardships and therefore returned to Makkah Mukarramah.

Lesson 6

When the Prophet ﷺ got back, he was, in bodily form, taken from Makkah Mukarramah to Jerusalem and from there onwards to the seven heavens and above. The Prophet ﷺ was also given 5 prayers as a gift. The first and second pledge of 'Aqabah also took place after this time. The Prophet then migrated to Madinah Munawwarah when he was 53 years old. The rulings of Zakaah, Sawm, and Hajj were given in Madinah Munawwarah after migration.

Lesson 7

The Prophet ﷺ stayed in Madinah Munawwarah for 10 years and 2 months and passed away just before noon on Rabee 'Ul-Awwal 11 Hijri, June 634 A.D. at the age of 63 years and 3 months. He was buried in 'Aishah's (RADH) room. Jibraeel (AS) and all the angels performed Janaazah salaah and then the household of the Prophet ﷺ and thereafter the Sahaabah (RADH) and then the women and children. The Prophet ﷺ was buried on Tuesday night.

Lesson 8

The 4 Khalifah (Khulafa Rashideen):

1. Abu Bakr Siddeeq (RADH) became the Khalifah after the demise of the Prophet ﷺ because he is the best person after the prophets. He served his post for over 2 years and passed away in 13th Hijri. He was buried next to the Prophet ﷺ. He was also the first man to accept Islam.

2. 'Umar bin Khattab (RADH) became the second Khalifah. He ruled for 10 years until he was martyred in 24th Hijri. He was 62 years old at the time of his death. 'Umar (RA) was also buried next to the Prophet ﷺ.

3. 'Uthman bin 'Affaan (RADH) was the third Khalifah of Islam and he made the first official copy of the Quran. He ruled for 11 years until he was also martyred in the 35th Hijri. He is buried in Jannatul Baqee', the graveyard of Madinah Munawwarah.

4. 'Ali bin Abu Talib (RADH) became the third Khalifah after the martyrdom of 'Uthman (RADH). He ruled for 5 years. He was martyred when he was 58 years old in 40th Hijri. His grave is in Kufah, Iraq. He was also the first boy to accept Islam.

Lesson 9

After the martyrdom of 'Ali (RADH), many Khalifahs came and went. The order of these Khalifahs is as follows:

1. Hasan bin 'Ali (RADH)
2. Mu'awiyah bin Abu Sufyan (RADH)
3. Yazeed bin Mu'awiyah
4. Mu'awiyah bin Yazeed
5. 'Abdullah bin Zubair (RADH)
6. Marwaan bin Hakam
7. 'Abdul Malik bin Marwaan
8. Waleed bin 'Abdul Malik
9. Sulaymaan bin 'Abdul Malik
10. 'Umar bin 'Abdul 'Aziz, who held the Khilafah for over 2 years; he passed away in 101 Hijri. His grave is in Homs (Syria).

The Messenger of Allah ﷺ said: *"The best of my nation is my generation, then those who follow them and then those who follow them."* [Bukhaari]

Lesson 10

'Asharatul Mubassharah:

Nabi ﷺ gave glad tidings of Jannah to these ten Sahaabah in one sitting. They were:

1. Abu Bakr Siddeeq (RADH) Father-in-law of Nabi ﷺ
2. 'Umar bin Khattab (RADH) Father-in-law of Nabi ﷺ
3. 'Uthman bin 'Affaan (RADH) Son-in-law of Nabi ﷺ
4. 'Ali bin Abu Talib (RADH) Cousin and Son-in-law of Nabi ﷺ
5. 'Abdur Rahman bin 'Awf (RADH)
6. Abu 'Ubaidah bin Jarraah (RADH)
7. Sa'd bin Abi Waqqaas (RADH)
8. Sa'eed bin Zaid (RADH)
9. Talha bin 'Ubaidullah (RADH)
10. Zubair bin 'Awwaam (RADH)

Lesson 11

Ashaabus Suffah (The People of the Platform):

The Ashaabus Suffah were poor companions of Nabi ﷺ who dedicated their lives exclusively for prayer, spiritual discipline and learning the Ahaadeeth in the close company of Nabi ﷺ. They were hundreds in number.

Some of the companions who were, at any one point, members of the Ashaabus Suffah were:

- Abu Hurairah (RADH)
- Abu Dharr Ghifari (RADH)
- 'Ammaar bin Yaasir (RADH)
- Khabbaab bin Aratt (RADH)
- Salmaan Faarsi (RADH)
- Hudhaifah bin Yamaan (RADH)
- 'Abdullah bin Mas'ood (RADH)
- 'Abdullah bin 'Umar (RADH)
- Suhayb bin Sinaan Roomi (RADH)
- Bilaal bin Rabaah (RADH) - He was the first slave to accept Islam.

THE AHLUL BAYT
(FAMILY TREE OF NABI ﷺ)

Lesson 12

Father: 'Abdullah bin 'Abdul Muttalib
Mother: Aaminah bint Wahb

Blessed Lineage:

Muhammad ﷺ bin (son of) 'Abdullah bin 'Abdul Muttalib bin Haashim bin 'Abd Manaaf bin Qusayy bin Kilaab bin Murrah bin Ka'b bin Lu-ayy bin Ghaalib bin Fihr (Quraysh) bin Maalik bin Nadhr bin Kinaanah bin Khuzaimah bin Mudrikah bin Ilyaas bin Mudhar bin Nizaar bin Ma'ad bin 'Adnaan.

'Adnaan was from the progeny of the prophet Ismaa'eel (AS), the son of the prophet Ibraheem (AS).

Lesson 13

Paternal Grandfather: 'Abdul Muttalib - His real name was Shaybah bin Haashim.
Paternal Grandmother: Fatimah bint 'Amr
Maternal Grandfather: Wahb bin 'Abd Manaaf
Maternal Grandmother: Barrah bint 'Abdul 'Uzza

Paternal Uncles: Nabi ﷺ had 12 paternal uncles.

1. Haarith - The eldest son of 'Abdul Muttalib and Samraa bint Jundub.
2. Quthum - The son of 'Abdul Muttalib and Samraa bint Jundub who passed away in his childhood.
3. Zubair - The son of 'Abdul Muttalib and Fatimah bint 'Amr and father of 'Abdullah bin Zubair (RADH), Umme Hakam (RADH), and Dhuba'a.
4. Abu Talib - The son of 'Abdul Muttalib and Fatimah bint 'Amr and father of Talib, 'Ali (RADH), 'Aqeel (RADH), Ja'far (RADH), and Umme Haani (RADH), whose real name was Faakhitah or Hind. His real name was 'Abd Manaf.
5. Abu Lahab - The son of 'Abdul Muttalib and Lubnaa bint Haajar and father of 'Utaybah, 'Utbah (RADH), Mu'attib (RADH), and Durra (RADH). His real name was 'Abdul 'Uzza.
6. Dhiraar - The son of 'Abdul Muttalib and Nukhaylah bint Janaab.
7. 'Abbas (RADH) - The son of 'Abdul Muttalib and Nukhaylah bint Janaab and he had ten sons of which were 'Abdullah bin 'Abbas (RADH), Fadhl (RADH), and Quthum (RADH). He passed away in the year 32 AH.
8. Hamzah (RADH) - The son of 'Abdul Muttalib and Haalah bint Wuhayb and father of Ammaarah (RADH). He is also the maternal cousin and foster brother of Nabi ﷺ. He was known as the lion of Islam and he is the leader of the Martyrs. He was martyred in the battle of Uhud.
9. Hajl - The son of 'Abdul Muttalib and Haalah bint Wuhayb. His real name was Mughirah.
10. Muqawwim - The son of 'Abdul Muttalib and Haalah bint Wuhayb.
11. 'Abdul Ka'bah
12. Ghidaaq

Paternal Aunts: Nabi ﷺ had 6 paternal aunts.
1. Safiyyah (RADH) - The daughter of 'Abdul Muttalib and Haalah bint Wuhayb and mother of Zubair bin 'Awwaam (RADH).
2. 'Aatikah - The daughter of 'Abdul Muttalib and Fatimah bint 'Amr.
3. Arwaa - The daughter of 'Abdul Muttalib and Fatimah bint 'Amr and mother of Tulayb (RADH).
4. Umaymah - The daughter of 'Abdul Muttalib and Fatimah bint 'Amr and mother of Zaynab bint Jahsh (RADH).
5. Barrah - The daughter of 'Abdul Muttalib and Fatimah bint 'Amr and mother of Abu Salamah (RADH), who was the first husband of Umme Salamah (RADH).
6. Umme Hakeem - The daughter of 'Abdul Muttalib and Fatimah bint 'Amr and maternal grandmother of 'Uthman (RADH). Her real name was Baydaa.

Lesson 14

Foster Mother: Haleemah Sa'diyyah (RADH)

Wet Nurses:
1. Umme Ayman (RADH) - Her real name was Barakah bint Tha'labah.
2. Thuwaybah (RADH) - She was the servant of Abu Lahab.

Foster Siblings:
1. Hamzah bin 'Abdul Muttalib (RADH) - He was breastfed by Thuwaybah.
2. Abu Salamah bin 'Abdul Asad Makhzoomi (RADH) - He was breastfed by Thuwaybah.
3. 'Abdullah bin Haarith - Son of Haleemah Sa'diyyah
4. Shaymah bint Haarith - Daughter of Haleemah Sa'diyyah
5. Aneesah bint Haarith - Daughter of Haleemah Sa'diyyah

Lesson 15

Pure Wives:

Muhammad ﷺ had 11 wives total; 2 passed away during his lifetime and he had 9 at the time of his death. They are the mothers of the believers.

1. Khadijah bint Khuwaylid (RADH) - She was the first woman to accept Islam and she passed away around ten years after prophethood.
2. Saudah bint Zam'ah (RADH) - She passed away in Dhul-Hijjah in the year 23 AH.
3. 'Aishah (RADH) Daughter of Abu Bakr Siddeeq (RADH) - She passed away in the year 57 AH at the age of 66.
4. Hafsah (RADH) Daughter of 'Umar bin Khattab (RADH) - She passed away in the year 40 AH at the age of 60.
5. Zaynab bint Khuzaymah (RADH) - She was known as Ummul Masaakeen, due to her generosity and she passed away two or three months after marriage in the year 3 AH at the age of 30.
6. Umme Salamah bint Abu Umayyah (RADH) - Her real name was Hind and she passed away in the year 62 AH at the age of 84.
7. Zaynab bint Jahsh (RADH) - She was known as Ummul Hakam and her original name was Barrah and she was the paternal cousin of Rasulullah ﷺ and she passed away in the year 20 AH at the age of 50 or 53.
8. Juwayriyah bint Haarith (RADH) - She passed away in the year 50 AH at the age of 65.
9. Umme Habeebah (RADH) Daughter of Abu Sufyan (RADH) - Her real name was Ramlah and she passed away in the year 44 AH at the age of 74.
10. Safiyyah bint Huyayy (RADH) - Her real name was Zaynab and she passed away in Ramadhan in the year 50 AH and she was originally Jewish.
11. Maymunah bint Haarith (RADH) - She passed away in the year 51 AH.

Female Servants:

1. Maariah Qibtiyyah (RADH) - She passed away in the year 16 AH.
2. Rayhaanah bint Sham'oon (RADH) - She passed away in the year 10 AH.
3. Nafeesah (RADH)

Lesson 16

Children:

The mother of all his children was Khadijah (RADH) except Ibraheem (RADH), whose mother was Maariah Qibtiyyah (RADH). In total, Rasulullah ﷺ had 7 children; 3 sons and 4 daughters.

1. Qaasim (RADH) - Rasulullah's ﷺ first child and passed away at the age of two. One of Rasulullah's ﷺ nicknames was Abul Qaasim.

2. 'Abdullah (RADH) - He was also known as Tayyib and Taahir.

3. Ibraheem (RADH) - Rasulullah's ﷺ last child and he was born in the year 8 AH and passed away in the year 10 AH, while he was 15-16 months old.

4. Zaynab (RADH) - Rasulullah's ﷺ first daughter born ten years before prophethood. She was married to Abul 'Aas (RADH), her maternal cousin, and had one son and one daughter and she passed away in the year 8 AH.

5. Ruqayyah (RADH) - The first wife of 'Uthman bin 'Affaan (RADH) and they had one son. She was originally married to 'Utbah bin Abu Lahab before being divorced. She passed away while the muslims were in the battle of Badr.

6. Umme Kulthoom (RADH) - The second wife of 'Uthman bin 'Affaan (RADH) and they had no children. She was originally married to 'Utaybah bin Abu Lahab before being divorced. She passed away in Sha'baan in the year 9 AH.

7. Fatimah (RADH) - The leader of the women in Paradise and the wife of 'Ali bin Abu Talib (RADH) and they had three sons and two daughters. Rasulullah's ﷺ lineage only continued from her children and she passed away in Ramadhan in the year 11 AH.

Adopted Son: Zaid bin Haarithah (RADH) - He married Umme Ayman (RADH) and they had one son, Usaamah bin Zaid (RADH).

Lesson 17

Grandchildren:

Children of Zaynab (RADH):
1. 'Ali bin Abul 'Aas (RADH)
2. Umaamah bint Abul 'Aas (RADH)

Children of Ruqayyah (RADH):
1. 'Abdullah bin 'Uthman (RADH) - He passed away at the age of 6.

Children of Fatimah (RADH):
1. Hasan bin 'Ali (RADH)
2. Husain bin 'Ali (RADH)
3. Muhsin bin 'Ali (RADH) - He passed away in infancy.
4. Zaynab bint 'Ali (RADH)
5. Umme Kulthoom bint 'Ali (RADH)

The Messenger of Allah ﷺ said: *"O people, I have left among you something of such a nature that if you adhere to it you will not go astray: Allah's Book and my close relatives who belong to my household."* [Tirmidhi]

Lesson 18

Characteristics and Appearance:
- His face shone like the full moon. He was average, not too short or tall.
- He had a broad forehead. He had fine hair on his eyebrows.
- His hair was slightly curled. His hair naturally parted in the middle. His hair used to pass over his earlobes.
- Both eyebrows were separate and did not meet. There was a vein between them, which used to expand when he became angry.
- His beard was full and dense. The pupils of his eyes were black.
- He had a luminous complexion. His nose was prominent and had Noor. His mouth was moderately wide.

- His cheeks were smooth and full of flesh. His cheeks were beautiful and thin.
- His teeth were thin and bright; the front teeth had a slight gap.
- All parts of his body were of a moderate size and fully fleshed.
- His body was proportionately joint. The bones of his joints were strong and large.
- His chest and stomach were in line, but his chest and shoulders were wide.
- Both sides, the shoulders and the upper portion of the chest, had hair.
- His forearms were long and palms wide. The palms and the feet were fully fleshed.
- The fingers and the toes were moderately long. The soles of his feet were a bit deep.
- When he walked, he put his feet softly on the ground. He walked at a quick pace.
- When he looked at something, he turned his whole body. His habit was to look at something with a light gaze.
- His sight was focused more on the ground than on the sky. He always kept his gaze down.
- He used to make Salaam first to whomsoever he met.

Lesson 19

Some Sunnah Food and Drinks:

1) Honey
2) Black Cumin (Kalunji)
3) Pumpkin
4) Meat
5) White (fine) Flour
6) Dates
7) Watermelons
8) Cucumber
9) Vinegar
10) Olives
11) Figs
12) Beetroot
13) Pears
14) Oranges
15) Pomegranate
16) Milk
17) Hareera (Talbeenah: mixture of barley, milk and honey)

Lesson 20

Some Sunnah Clothes and Applications:

1) White coloured clothes
2) Qamees/Tunic
3) Hibarah (Yemeni Blanket)
4) Lungi
5) Roomi Jabbah (Robe)
6) 'Imaamah (Turban) - Black/White
7) Qalansuwah (Cap/Topi)
8) Leather socks
9) Ithmid Kuhl (Surma, antimony)
10) Perfume - 'Itr/Musk/Amber/Oudh
11) Henna
12) Olive Oil
13) Comb
14) Ring
15) Mudd
16) Miswaak

Lesson 21

Some Miracles:

1) Splitting of the moon in half
2) Slitting of the blessed heart
3) Water gushing out from between the fingers
4) Informing about the Baitul Maqdis
5) The tree informing about the Jinns
6) One cup of milk sufficient for all
7) Walking past the non-believers without them knowing
8) The horse of Suraaqah sinking in the ground
9) A rock presenting itself after the Prophet's call
10) The Prophet's vision of the front and behind
11) The presence of the angels in the battle of Badr
12) Tree giving shade to the Prophet and saying salaam
13) Camel obeying the orders of the Prophet
14) Informing about the martyrs of the battle of Mu-tah
15) Trees and mountains saying salaam to the Prophet

Lesson 22

Ghazawaat (Ghazwah) are those battles and expeditions led by Nabi.

Saraayah (Sariyyah) are those expeditions that were dispatched and sent by Nabi.

There were a total of 28 Ghazawaat and 46 Saraayah.

Famous Ghazawaat of Islam:
1. The Battle of Badr - Ramadhan 2 AH -
2. The Battle of Uhud - Shawwaal 3 AH
3. The Battle of Khandaq (Trench)/ Ahzaab (Confederates) - Shawwaal 5 AH
4. The Treaty of Hudaybiyah - Dhul-Qa'dah 6 AH
5. The Battle of Khaybar - 7 AH
6. The Conquest of Makkah - Ramadhan 8 AH
7. The Battle of Hunayn - Shawwaal 8 AH
8. The Battle of Tabuk - Rajab 9 AH

Famous Saraayah of Islam:
1. Saiful Bahr
2. Bir Ma'oonah - 4 AH
3. Fidak
4. Dawmatul Jundal
5. Mu-tah - Jumaadal-Oola 8 AH

Lesson 23

THE LAST SERMON OF THE PROPHET MUHAMMAD ﷺ

The Last Sermon of the Prophet ﷺ was during the farewell Hajj (Hajjatul Wadaa') Dhul-Hijjah 10th AH on the plains of 'Arafah in front of 140,000 Sahaabah. After praising and thanking Allah, the Prophet said, "Oh people, listen to my words carefully for I know not whether I will meet you on such an occasion again."

DO NOT OPPRESS EACH OTHER

'Beware! The blood and property of the Muslim is sacred, just as this day, month and city are sacred. And beware, I will reach the pond of Kawther before you and will be proud in front of the other nations because of you. So do not blacken my face, do not disgrace me. And beware, I will save some of you, and others will be far away from me...I will say; O my Lord these are my companions... Allah will say: 'You are not aware of the fact that they made changes to that which you left with them.' (Ibn Majah)

FINANCIAL OBLIGATIONS AND TRUST

'If anybody is made custodian of anything, he must keep that trust till the thing held in custody is restored to the rightful owner.' (Muslim)

INTEREST (RIBA)

'Beware! Remember all the matters related to the time of ignorance have been placed under my feet and the monetary interest of that time has also been canceled. (Muslim)

FAIR TREATMENT OF WIFE (SPOUSE)

'Fear Allah with regards to your women. You have made them halal for you with the name of Allah.' (Muslim)

WARNING ABOUT SHAYTAAN

'The Devil (Shaytaan) has conceded that he will not be worshiped in this land of yours. (Worshiping idols in this Hijaaz) However, the Devil is happy that he can mislead you with other sins.' (Musnad Ahmad)

BROTHERHOOD OF MUSLIMS

'Know that every Muslim is a brother to another Muslim and that the Mus-lims are brothers, therefore no man should have access to his brother's wealth, unless with his goodwill.' (Tirmidhi)

PREVENTING EVIL

'If any of you see an evil act being performed, he should prevent it with his hand, if he does not have the power to do this, then he should do so with his tongue, if that too is not possible, then he should think bad of it in his heart. And this is the weakest level of Imaan (faith). (Muslim)

SUPERIORITY IS ONLY IN PIETY AND SUBMISSION

'The Arab is not superior to a non-Arab, neither a non-Arab to an Arab, neither a red-skinned person to a black-skinned person and neither a black-skinned person to a red-skinned person, except through taqwa.' (Musnad Ahmad)

HOLD ONTO THE QURAN AND SUNNAH TO BE SUCCESSFUL

'O people! I am leaving with you such things that if you hold fast to them you will never go astray, they are the book of Allah (Quran) and my Sunnah.' (Tirmidhi)

OBSERVE THE PILLARS OF ISLAM

'Fear your Lord Allah, read the 5 daily Salaah, keep the fasts of Ramadhan, give Zakaah from your wealth, perform Hajj to the House of Allah, obey those in positions of leadership, and thus you shall enter your Lord's paradise.' (Tirmidhi)

DUTIES REGARDING THOSE WORKING UNDER US

'Take care of your slaves. Let them eat what you yourself eat and let them wear as you wear yourself.' (Muslim)

HAVING CONCERN FOR THE HEREAFTER

'Whosoever has the concern of the hereafter, Allah makes his difficulties easy and the Dunya (world) itself will come to them humiliated. And whosoever has the concern for this world, Allah will increase his difficulties and make poverty their condition. Only that amount of wealth can be attained which is preordained by Allah!' (Tabraani)

MUHAMMAD IS THE LAST PROPHET

'There will be no prophet after me and no nation after you.' (Bukhaari)

OUR DUTY IS TO SPREAD THE MESSAGE OF THE PROPHET (QURAN)

'Listen! Those who are present here should convey my message to others not present here.' (Bukhaari)

Then the Prophet ﷺ asked the audience, "Have I conveyed the Message of Allah to you?"

The audience answered in one voice, "We bear witness that you have conveyed the message, discharged your duty, and advised us."

Thereupon Allah's Messenger lifted his forefinger towards the sky and then pointing towards people said, "Be my witness O Allah, that I have conveyed Your message to Your people."

ACTIVITIES

1) When was Prophet Muhammad ﷺ born? Explain the whole incident before his birth and design a poster. The whole story is mentioned in Surah Feel.

2) Draw a family tree of the Prophet ﷺ and write down his whole family from grandfather to grandchildren. There should be up to 55 names!

3) Give the Prophet's ﷺ lineage up to his fifth ancestor.

4) Shaqqus Sadr (splitting of the chest) took place on a few occasions during the Prophet's ﷺ life. Please explain the occasions in detail.

5) The Prophet ﷺ traveled to Syria for business trips. Who did he travel with? Mention the whole incident that took place there along with the Christian monk's name who recognized that Muhammad ﷺ was going to be a Prophet.

6) Write what happened when the Prophet was 6, 8, 12 and 35 years old?

7) What was the name of the Christian monk who recognized that Muhammad ﷺ was going to be a Prophet?

8) What was the first revelation and where was it revealed? Mention the whole incident and also what words Khadijah (RADH) said to confront her husband.

9) What is the Pledge of 'Aqabah? Explain its significance and how many people took part.

10) What is the name of the whole journey to the seven heavens and how did the whole journey take place? Please explain in detail. You may draw the map too.

11) Mention the incident of Hijrah and how it took place?

12) Who are the Ansaar and Muhaajiroon?

13) What were the two main tribes living in Madinah Munawwarah when our Beloved Prophet ﷺ migrated from Makkah Mukarramah to Madinah Munawwarah?

14) Which beloved uncle of the Prophet ﷺ was martyred in the battle of Uhud and what was his title?

15) Explain briefly the battles of Badr and Uhud. You may draw a diagram showing the whole battlefield. Write when it took place and how many people were involved in each. Also mention the virtues for taking part.

16) Name the two wives of the Prophet ﷺ who were daughters of the first two companions of the Prophet ﷺ.

17) Who was the first male, female, child, and slave to accept Islam?

18) Explain who a Sahaabi is and what happens to a person who disregards them?

19) Sit in a quiet place and visualize ALL the blessed features of the Prophet ﷺ and tell your teacher how you felt. You can do this together in class with your teacher.

20) Write down any 10 points you learnt from the Prophet's ﷺ farewell sermon. You can make a poster out of each point and stick it up in your classroom!

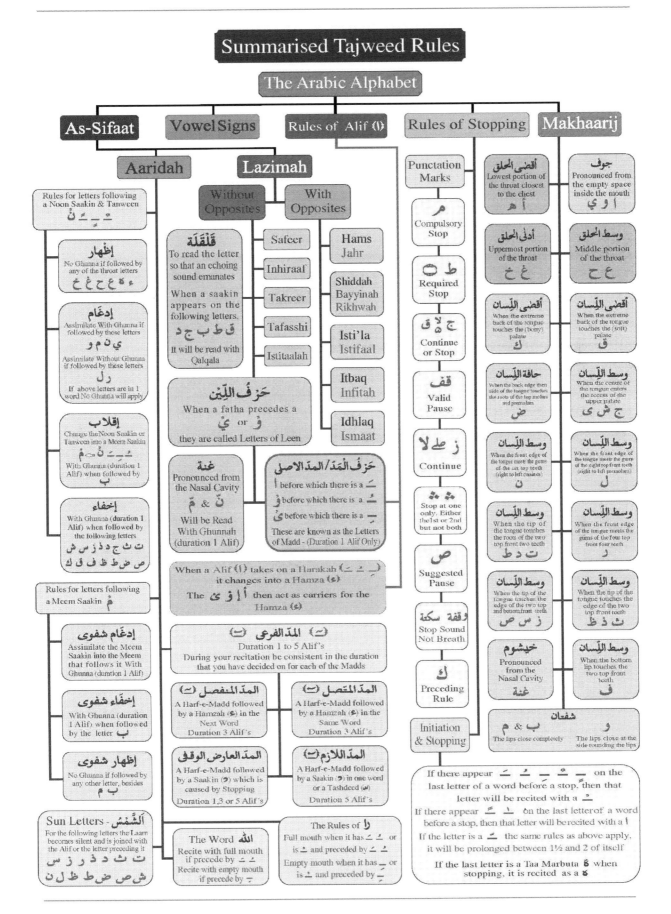

TAJWEED

Level 1

Definition: Tajweed means to recite every letter correctly, from its Makhraj (origin point) with all its qualities.

Status: It is Fardh (obligatory) to learn Tajweed in order to recite the Quran properly.

Aadaab of Reciting Quran:

1. To be clean and in the state of Wudhu.

2. To sit in front of the Quran with great respect and to refrain from those actions that are disrespectful.

3. To face the Qiblah whenever possible.

4. To place the Quran on something high, like a desk or stand.

5. To begin reading with Ta'awwudh and Tasmiyah.

6. To recite with full concentration and not allow other thoughts to enter the mind.

7. To refrain from unnecessary talking.

8. If one talks, they should recite Ta'awwudh before resuming.

9. The listener should listen with full attention.

10. The reciter should recite in a beautiful voice while fulfilling all the rules of Tajweed.

Makhaarij

The makhraj is like a launching pad for Arabic letters. It's the spot in our mouth or throat where each letter starts when we say it. When we learn the makhaarij, we can pronounce the letters correctly and recite the Quran with beautiful and accurate pronunciation. There are **17 Makhaarij** in total:

1. Emptiness of the mouth: ا و ى (**Maddah**)
   - The letters of **Madd** are pronounced from the empty space in the mouth.
2. The Bottom of the throat: ء ه
3. The Middle of the throat: ع ح
4. The Top of the throat: غ خ
5. ق is pronounced when the extreme back of the tongue touches the soft palate.
6. ك is pronounced when the back of the tongue touches the soft palate.
7. ج ش ي are pronounced when the center of the tongue touches the palate.
8. ض is pronounced when the upturned back edge of the tongue lifts and touches the root of the molars and premolars of the upper jaw.
9. ل is pronounced when the edge of the tongue meets the gums of the upper front eight teeth.
10. ن is pronounced when the edge of the tongue meets the gums of the upper front six teeth.
11. ر is pronounced when the edge of the tongue meets the gums of the upper front four teeth.
12. ت د ط are pronounced when the tip of the tongue touches the roots of the upper front two teeth.
13. ث ذ ظ are pronounced when the tip of the tongue touches the edge of the upper front two teeth.
14. ز س ص are pronounced when the tip of the tongue touches the inside edge of the bottom front two teeth.
15. ف is pronounced when the inner center of the bottom lip touches the edge of the upper front two teeth.

16. ب is pronounced from the wet portion of the lips and م is pronounced from the dry portion of the lips and و is pronounced from the incomplete meeting of the lips.
17. Ghunnah is pronounced from the Nostrils.

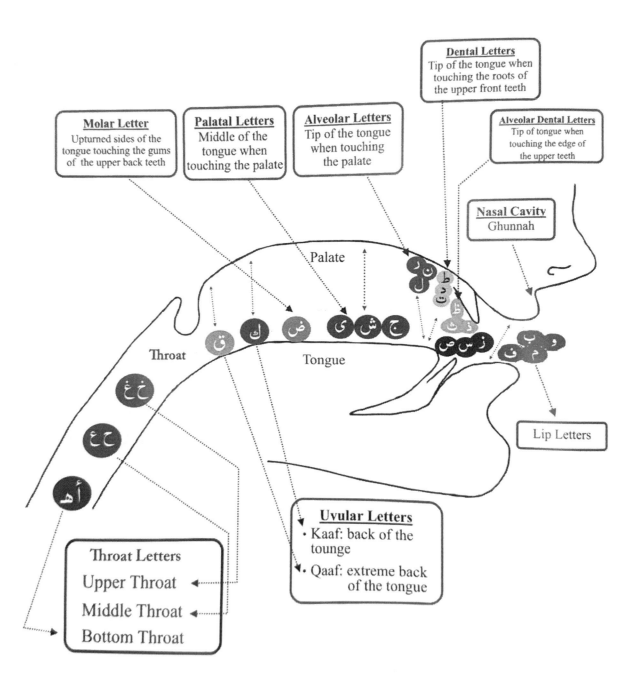

ا ب ت ث ج ح خ د ذ ر ز
س ش ص ض ط ظ ع غ
ف ق ك ل م ن و ء ه ي

Rules of Full Mouth & Empty Mouth

There are seven 7 letters that are always read with a Full mouth.
There are three 3 letters that are sometimes read with a Full mouth and sometimes with an Empty mouth. ا (Empty Alif) ل and ر
The remaining nineteen 19 letters will always be read with an Empty mouth.

The Full Mouth Letters: خ ص ض غ ط ظ ق

- These letters will always be read with Full mouth. خُصَّ ضَغْطٍ قِظْ is what they are known as collectively. خَلَقَ ، أَنْقَضَ ظَهْرَكَ

The Empty Alif: ا

- If an Empty Alif comes after one of the seven Full mouth letters, then the Empty Alif will also be with a Full mouth. وَلَا الضَّآلِّينَ
- If an Empty Alif comes after one of the Empty mouth letters, then the Empty Alif will also be read with an Empty mouth. العَالَمِينَ

The Laam of Allah: الله

- If before the word الله appears a Zabar (َ) or Pesh (ُ), then you will read it with Full mouth. عِنْدَ اللهِ ، وَ اذْكُرُوا اللهَ
- If before the word الله appears a Zer (ِ), then you will read it with Empty mouth. قُلِ اللَّهُمَّ

The Letter ر:

- If the letter ر has a Zabar (َ) or Pesh (ُ), then you will read it with Full mouth, and if it has a Zer (ِ), you will read it with Empty mouth. رَبَّنَا ، رُسُلٌ ، رِجَالٌ
- The same rule will be applied even if the letter ر has a Tashdeed (ّ). حَرَّمَ اللهُ ، يَمُرُّونَ ، مِنْ شَرٍّ
- If the letter ر has a Sukoon (ْ), then you will read it according to the Harakat of the letter before it. تَرْتِيلًا ، تُرْجَعُونَ ، يَسْتَغْفِرْ لَكُمْ
- The same rule will be applied even if you stop on the ر (do Waqf). وَالْعَصْرِ ، مِنْ نُورٍ ، لِذِيْ حِجْرٍ

Exceptional cases where you do not follow the above rules:

- If you are doing Waqf on ر and before it is a يْ, then you will always read it with Empty mouth, regardless of the Harakat of the letter before it. لَا ضَيْرَ
- If the رْ Saakin has a Full mouth letter after it, then you will read it with Full mouth, regardless of the Harakat of the letter before it. مِرْصَادًا
- If the letter ر comes after a temporary Zer (ِ), then you will read it with Full mouth. اِرْجِعِيْ
- If the رْ Saakin has a Zer (ِ) before it, but it is in the previous word (not in the same word), then you will read it with a Full mouth. رَبِّ ارْجِعُونَ

Qalqalah: ق ط ب ج د

- If there is a Sukoon (ْ) on any of these 5 letters, they will be read with an echo or bouncing sound. قُطْبُ جَدٍّ is what they are known as collectively. يَجْعَلُ ، فَارْغَبْ

Rules of Waqf (Stopping)

- When you do Waqf (stop) on a word, then all Harakaat (ُ , ِ , َ) besides double zabar and standing zabar, will be read as a Sukoon (ْ). حَكِيمٌ عَلِيْمٌ ، خُلُقٍ عَظِيمٍ ، هُمُ الصّٰدِقُونَ
- When you do Waqf on a round taa (ة), then it will be read as a (ه) Haa Saakin. نَخْلٍ خَاوِيَةٍ
- When you do Waqf on a Double Zabar (ً), then it will be read as a Zabar (َ) with Madd Asli. غَفُورًا رَحِيمًا
- When you do Waqf on an Empty Alif with a Zabar (َ) before it or an Empty Yaa ى with a Zabar (َ) before it, then this Zabar will be read with Madd Asli. ضُحٰهَا ، أَعْلٰى
- When you do Waqf on an Empty Yaa ى with a Standing Zabar (ٰ) before it, then no changes will be made. مُوْسٰى

Rules of Madd (Stretching)

The meaning of Madd is to prolong the letters from its original position. There are two types of Madd:
1. Madd Asli
2. Madd Far'ie

Madd Asli:

There are six cases of Madd Asli: (1) If there is an Empty alif ا with a Zabar (َ) before it, (2) or a Yaa Saakin ي with a Zer (ِ) before it, (3) or a Waw Saakin و with a Pesh (ُ) before it, (4) or a Standing Zabar (ٰ), (5) or a Standing Zer, (6) or an Inverted Pesh, then you will stretch the sound for the duration of one count. نُوْحِيْهَا ، أُوْذِيْنَا

Madd Leen:

There are two cases of Madd Leen: (1) If there is a Waw Saakin و with a Zabar (َ) before it, (2) or a Yaa Saakin ي with a Zabar (َ) before it, then it will be read quickly and clearly. كَوْثَرَ ، عَلَيْكُمْ

Madd Far'ie:

If there is a Hamzah ا / ء or Sukoon (ْ) after Madd Asli or Madd Leen, then it will be one of the five types of Madd Far'ie.

Madd Muttasil:

This is the first type of Madd Far'ie. If there is a Hamzah ء in the same word after Madd Asli, then you will stretch the sound for the duration of about four counts. جَاءَ ، اَلسُّوْءَ ، سِيْءَ

Madd Munfasil:

This is the second type of Madd Far'ie. If there is a Hamzah ا in the next word after Madd Asli, then you will stretch the sound for the duration of about three counts. كَمَآ أُمِرْتُ ، تُوْبُوْٓا إِلَيْهِ ، وَيَهْدِيْٓ إِلَيْهِ

Madd Laazim:

This is the third type of Madd Far'ie. If there is a Tashdeed or Sukoon after Madd Asli, then you will stretch the sound for the duration of five counts. وَلَا الضَّآلِّينَ ، اَلْئٰنَ

Madd Aaridh Waqfi:

This is the fourth type of Madd Far'ie. If there is a temporary Sukoon (due to stopping on the letter) after Madd Asli, then you will stretch the sound for the duration of about three counts. خَلَقَ الْإِنْسَانَ ، كُنْ فَيَكُوْنُ ، صِرَاطٍ مُسْتَقِيْمٍ

Madd Leen Aaridh Waqfi:

This is the fifth type of Madd Far'ie. If there is a temporary Sukoon (due to stopping on the letter) after the letters of Leen, then you will stretch the sound for the duration of about two counts. مِنْ خَوْفٍ ، وَالصَّيْفِ

Rules of Ghunnah

Waajib Ghunnah: نّ مّ (Ghunnah is Compulsory)

If there is a Noon or Meem with tashdeed مّ, then you must read it with Ghunnah. أَنَّا ، أَمَّا

Rules of Noon Saakin & Tanween: نْ / ً ٍ ٌ

Izhaar: (to make clear) ء ه ع ح غ خ

If after نْ or ً ٍ ٌ any of the 6 letters of Izhaar come, then you will read it clearly without Ghunnah. مِنْ أَهْلِ ، ذَرَّةٍ خَيْرًا

Iqlaab: (to convert) ب

If after نْ or ً ٍ ٌ the letter ب appears, then you will change the sound of نْ or ً ٍ ٌ into م and read it with Ghunnah. مِنْ م بَعْدِ ، يَوْمَئِذٍ م بِجَهَنَّمْ

Idghaam: (to merge)

With Ghunnah: ي م و ن

If after نْ or ً ٍ ٌ any of the 4 letters of Idghaam with Ghunnah appear, then you will read it with Ghunnah. فَمَنْ يَعْمَلْ ، خَيْرًا يَرَهْ

Without Ghunnah: ر ل

If after نْ or ً ٍ ٌ any of the 2 letters of Idghaam without Ghunnah appear, then you will read it clearly without Ghunnah. مِنْ رَبِّهِمْ ، كِتَابًا لَكُمْ

Ikhfaa: (to hide): ت ث ج د ذ ز س ش ص ض ط ظ ف ق ك

If after نْ or ً ٍ ٌ any of the 15 letters of Ikhfaa appear, then you will hide the sound of نْ or ً ٍ ٌ in the nose and read it with Ghunnah. مَنْ تَابَ ، خَيْرًا كَثِيرًا

Rules of Meem Saakin: مْ

Ikhfaa Shafawi: ب

If after مْ the letter ب appears, then you will read it with Ghunnah. رَّبُّهُمْ بِهِمْ

Idghaam Shafawi: م

If after مْ the letter م appears, then you will connect them together and read it with Ghunnah. لَهُمْ مَّغْفِرَةٌ

Izhaar Shafawi: any letter besides م ب

If after مْ any letters besides م ب appears, then you will read it clearly without Ghunnah. أَلَمْ يَجْعَلْ

وَرَتِّلِ ٱلْقُرْءَانَ تَرْتِيلًا

"And recite the Quran clearly with tarteel (in a distinct and measured tone)."

Made in the USA
Middletown, DE
29 June 2024

56489679R00071